D1194877

questions
practice

3+4

A Homestay in Japan

日本との出会い

A Homestay in Japan

NIHON TO NO DEAI

Intermediate Reader for Students of Japanese

CARON ALLEN WITH NATSUMI WATANABE

*Center for Improvement of Teaching
of Japanese Language and Culture in High School*
URBANA, ILLINOIS

Illustrations by Linda Duke

STONE BRIDGE PRESS

Berkeley, California

The Center for Improvement of Teaching of Japanese Language and Culture in High School develops teaching materials for the study of Japanese, publishes a newsletter for high school Japanese language teachers, conducts instructional programs for teachers, and provides assistance to schools implementing new programs in Japanese. Further information may be obtained from the Center for Improvement of Teaching of Japanese Language and Culture in High School, University of Illinois, University High School, 1212 West Springfield Avenue, Urbana, IL 61801. Telephone: 217-244-4808 or 217-333-8203.

Published by Stone Bridge Press, P.O. Box 8208, Berkeley, CA 94707.

Book design and composition by Tulip Graphics, Berkeley, California.

Printed in the United States of America.

10 9 8 7 6 5 4 3 2

Library of Congress Cataloging-in-Publication Data

Allen, Caron.
    A homestay in Japan: intermediate reader for students of Japanese / by Caron Allen with Natsumi Watanabe; with illustrations by Linda Duke.
        p.   cm.
    English and Japanese.
    ISBN 0-9628137-6-1 (softcover)
    ISBN 1-880656-03-5 (hardcover)
    1. Japanese language--Textbooks for foreign speakers--English. 2. Japanese language--Readers. I. Watanabe, Natsumi. II. Duke, Linda. III. Title.
    [PL539.5.E5A44   1992]
    495.6'86421--dc20
                                                    92-10662
                                                      CIP

CONTENTS

Teacher's Guide

A Homestay in Japan

Appendixes

Teacher's Guide

ACKNOWLEDGMENTS

A Homestay in Japan was created in response to the need for high-school-level Japanese-language teaching materials. Carol Bond, Director of The Center for Improvement of Teaching of Japanese Language and Culture in High School (University High School, Urbana, IL), along with her assistant, Barbara Shenk, laid the groundwork and lovingly guided this project from conception to birth. Coauthor Natsumi Watanabe provided her special blend of creativity, humor, and professionalism. *A Homestay in Japan* was generously funded by the Secretary's Discretionary Program for Critical Foreign Languages—U.S. Department of Education, the United States–Japan Foundation, and University High School (University of Illinois at Urbana-Champaign).

I would like to thank the following teachers and their students who kindly contributed their time and expertise to field-test an early draft of the book:

Leslie Birkland, Lake Washington High School, Kirkland, WA

Kim Parent, Arsenal Technical High School, Indianapolis, IN

Yoshio Satoh, Breck School, Golden Valley, MN

Masatoshi Shimano, St. Paul's School, Concord, NH

Raymond Stein, Mt. Edgecumbe High School, Sitka, AK

Michael Sudlow, North Salem High School, Salem, OR

Phyllis Larson and Takako Michii painstakingly and thoroughly reviewed this book. I am grateful for the comments and suggestions they provided.

I'd also like to express my appreciation to those many others who made valuable contributions to this book: Hiromi Hashida; Kazumi Hatasa; Taeko Horwitz; Taiji and Mayumi Hotta; Mariko Kaga; Sachiko Kaji; Akiko Kakutani; Takuo Kinoshita; Seiichi Makino; Amy Miller; Kate Okubo; David Plath; Keiko Sakui; Yoko Sugimura; Koji, Setsuko and Karl Taira; Christopher Thompson; Michio Tsutsui; and Michiko Uchiyama. Sherry Fink, Joe Grohens, and Vivian Shackelford provided patient and invaluable assistance with manuscript preparation.

I'd like to thank Linda Duke for the warmth and joy she expresses in her illustrations and Carol Bond for her incredible patience, inspiration, and hard work. And finally, thanks to my host family, the Kishimotos, and to all my friends in Japan and America for their kindness, love, and support.

Caron Allen

TEACHING WITH *A HOMESTAY IN JAPAN*

A Homestay in Japan was designed as a supplementary reader for high school students in their third or fourth year of Japanese-language instruction and has been successfully field-tested in a number of secondary schools throughout the United States. The book may also be adapted for use in introductory college courses. As a supporting teaching aid, its purpose is to develop reading proficiency and cultural understanding, to introduce new vocabulary, and to serve as a source for oral and written practice. The reader also demonstrates cultural aspects of communication, such as the subtle use (or lack of use) in daily life of the word for "no."

A Homestay in Japan relates the experiences of Amy, a sixteen-year-old American exchange student who spends a year living with a Japanese family in Kobe. Members of Amy's host family are Mr. Yamashita (a businessman), Mrs. Yamashita (a homemaker), and their children, Ichirō (age 16), Akiko (age 14), and Mayumi (age 5). It should be noted that because this is a language textbook, Amy's speech is fluent and correct even though she is unfamiliar with many aspects of Japanese culture. Likewise, the text is written in standard Japanese, rather than in a local or regional dialect.

Each of the twenty chapters combines both narrative and conversational styles. As students read conversations between Amy, her host family and others, they will encounter colloquial expressions, appropriate male and female speech markers, and varying speech styles and levels of formality. Students can thus experience the depth and richness of the Japanese language, as well as its use in context.

As they read, students will encounter familiar grammatical structures and kanji,

and will be introduced to new kanji and vocabulary:

(a) The grammatical structures used throughout the reader repeat and reinforce those already introduced in most Japanese texts currently in use in high school classes through the third year. Teachers should refer to the vocabulary list for each chapter, where key grammatical patterns are noted.

(b) Kanji are written with furigana throughout the chapter in which they first appear, unless they are among the most basic kanji typically introduced in the first year of Japanese instruction (such as the kanji for *Nihon, iku,* and *kuru*). A kanji that appears again in later units will not have furigana unless it is part of a new compound. For the teacher's reference, kanji are listed separately in this Teacher's Guide, by unit, in the order in which they first appear.

(c) New vocabulary is presented at the bottom of each page of the main text. Most vocabulary items are presented in dictionary form, along with the appropriate contextual English meaning.

It is not necessary for students to understand every word in order to benefit from reading. *A Homestay in Japan* can help students develop effective reading strategies so that they can grasp the main ideas of the text as well as many supporting details without resorting to translation. Students should be encouraged to skim a passage first to get the general sense or gist of the passage; to identify key sentences necessary to retell the main ideas of the story; to guess unfamiliar vocabulary words from context; to recognize which words they should look up and which words they can comfortably ignore; and to scan for details (for example, to locate answers to specific questions). They should then reread the passage for fuller comprehension. For a very readable discussion of the process of teaching reading comprehension, teachers should refer to Alice Omaggio's excellent book, *Teaching Language in Context: Proficiency-Oriented Instruction* (Heinle & Heinle Publishers, 1986).

In using *A Homestay in Japan* to develop reading proficiency, the prereading and postreading strategies described below will greatly enhance interest, understanding, and enjoyment of the text.

Prereading Phase

The main goal of the prereading phase is to facilitate reading comprehension by encouraging students to form basic assumptions about a text before they actually read it. This preparatory work can be carried out in a variety of ways using the following features of the reader:

1. *Cast of Characters and Basic Premise.* At the outset, teachers might wish to explain the premise of the book to their students. Or, they might ask their students to scan the Table of Contents and then speculate about the characters and the story. For example, the class can be asked to imagine Mr. Yamashita's daily schedule, his role in the family, and what level of language he might use with his wife and children or with Amy. Students should be encouraged to base their responses on what they have already learned about Japanese family life. Asking students to express their own feelings and opinions is also an important part of reading preparation. For example, prior to reading Unit 1, students could be asked how they would feel if they were about to meet their Japanese host family for the first time or what they would want to say to their family.

2. *Illustrations.* Near the beginning of each chapter is an illustration of a scene from the story. During the prereading phase, students can anticipate the setting or plot by carefully examining visual clues provided in the illustrations. The illustrations will also help students learn vocabulary and can later serve as a source for discussion or a descriptive writing assignment. By incorporating additional visual aids, teachers can further enhance vocabulary acquisition as well as comprehension of the text and the cultural information it conveys.

3. *Culture Notes.* Following most chapters is a set of brief culture notes which serve to introduce aspects of Japanese life that may be unfamiliar to many young Americans. The culture notes are not meant to provide comprehensive information. Rather, they are short, descriptive pieces upon which the teacher is free to expand, according to individual needs and interests. The notes can be used as a starting point for class discussions, or to introduce a chapter. A list of suggested books for further study is sometimes included. In the vocabulary lists, an asterisk after a vocabulary item means "refer to the culture notes."

Postreading Activities

After reading the text of each unit, students can do exercises and activities to check comprehension and to involve themselves further in the material.

1. *Exercises.* Following each chapter is a set of exercises designed to aid in reading comprehension and cultural understanding. The first of these present simple, short-answer and true-false questions to verify student comprehension of basic content and meaning. A second set of questions relates the student's own experience and opinions to the content of each chapter. By formulating personalized responses to these questions, each student has the opportunity to become more engaged in the learning process.

2. *Activities.* The section "Classroom Activities" offers practical ideas designed to involve the student actively in the process of developing intercultural understanding. For example, students might be asked to role-play, to prepare Japanese food, or to reenact a scene from the reader. These classroom activities encourage students to discover and explore their own responses to a new situation. The use of English or Japanese is unspecified in some activities so that teachers can adapt them to the varying language abilities of their students. In either language, the activities are valuable for the cultural knowledge they impart.

*   *   *

A Homestay in Japan offers two unique features that set it apart from most Japanese textbooks. First, it presents a personalized picture of Japanese language and culture based on a young American's real-life experiences in Japan. Second, it offers a special glimpse into everyday aspects of Japanese life that are not typically included in most language textbooks. As students are enticed to explore the complexity and beauty of another language and culture, as well as their own, they will begin to discover the endless adventures possible when the two cultures meet.

CLASSROOM ACTIVITIES

Unit 1

1. Design a role-play activity in which small groups of students reenact the scene where Amy first meets her host family. Have the students take turns playing different roles.

2. Ask your students to make a list of the things they might want to take with them for a year-long stay in Japan as an exchange student. This can be done as a group, in pairs, or by individuals. As an alternative, set a limit on the number of items that may be taken, and ask students to explain their choices.

3. Together with your students, locate Kobe on a map. Bring in slides, books, travel brochures, or travel guides featuring Kobe to familiarize students with the setting.

Unit 2

1. Arrange to make *soba* for your class. Demonstrate how to use chopsticks so students can slurp their noodles in the Japanese manner. A recipe for *zaru soba* may be found on page 173, or refer to *The Book of Soba*, cited in Unit 5 Culture Notes.

2. Ask students to describe American eating customs that might seem unusual to a Japanese student visiting the U.S.

Unit 3

1. Help your students become aware of the differences and similarities between Japanese and American hospitality. Ask your students to imagine what their own family might do to welcome a foreign guest their age, and then compare these plans with the welcome the Yamashitas prepared for Amy.

2. Show slides and pictures of Japanese homes to your class. Try to include ex-

amples of both exterior and interior views and both Japanese- and Western-style rooms. Include examples of *genkan*, *tokonoma*, *futon*, and *tatami*. Use these visual aids to help your students compare Japanese and American housing. For example, note exterior features such as walls, fences, lawns, gardens, and gates and interior features such as floors, arrangement and type of furniture, storage space, beds, bathrooms, and kitchens.

3. Bring adzuki beans to class so that students can see what the filling for Amy's pillow is like.

Unit 4

1. Ask your students to invent a Japanese host family with whom they might like to stay. Ask them to write a description of each family member and list what *miyage* they would bring that person. As an alternative, have one group of students "create" a host family and another group decide what *miyage* to bring them.

2. Ask students how they might describe American gift-giving customs to a Japanese exchange student. Then discuss the importance of gift-giving and gift-wrapping in Japan. Demonstrate how to wrap and present a gift.

3. Ask your students to bring a picture of their own family to class and tell their host family (portrayed by fellow classmates) about themselves and each member of their family. If students have a hobby, ask them to bring some representative object such as a stamp book or a set of baseball cards to class as well. Their "host family" can then ask questions about their hobby.

4. Prepare *kuri manjū* with your class (see page 174 for the recipe). Or select another sweet from one of the cookbooks

listed in Unit 5 Culture Notes, or perhaps one of your own favorites.

Unit 5

1. Prepare a traditional Japanese breakfast with rice, miso soup, and pickles. If possible, use proper dishes—a ceramic bowl for rice and a lacquered bowl for soup. (Asian grocery stores often sell inexpensive, imitation lacquered bowls.)

2. Suggest that students try the following experiment: Get two pairs of slippers, one to be kept in the bathroom at home and a separate pair for the rest of the house. Wear these in the home as the Japanese might do. In other words, street shoes should be removed just inside the entry of the house and the slippers worn in the hallways and rooms that are not covered with "tatami" (select a carpeted room to serve as a tatami room). After a few days, students should write about or discuss their experience.

Unit 6

1. As a long-term assignment, have the class plan an armchair tour of a Japanese city. Assign small groups of students to research topics such as population, climate, housing, transportation, landmarks, specialty foods, commerce, and festivals. Help them obtain pictures, slides, maps, and travel brochures.

2. Ask class members to imagine they are living in the city they researched. Ask them to write a simple letter in Japanese, describing the city and what it is like to live there.

3. Have students write a letter describing their own town or community to a "pen pal" in Japan. As an alternative, ask them to sketch a series of "postcards" or to design a travel brochure of their own community with captions in Japanese.

Unit 7

1. Bring pictures to class of a variety of objects found in Japanese department stores. A gift catalog from a Japanese department store is useful for this project.

2. Prepare "yen notes" and have your class use them to practice buying store goods.

Unit 8

Use pictures illustrating Japanese bathing customs to generate a discussion of bathing practices in both America and Japan. Excellent sources for such pictures are the books *A Day in the Life of Japan* and *Pleasures of the Japanese Bath* (see Resources for Teaching about Japan and Unit 8 Culture Notes).

Unit 9

1. Divide the students into pairs. Ask one student to play the role of a Japanese student and the other, an American. The Japanese student must explain to the American student how to take a Japanese-style bath. Then, reverse the situation and ask the American student to explain an American-style bath or shower.

2. Demonstrate how to tie a *furoshiki*. Then ask for volunteers to try doing it.

Unit 10

1. For students interested in corresponding with a Japanese pen pal, information may be obtained from the International Friendship Club, P.O. Box 6 Hatogaya, Saitama 334, Japan.

2. Give each student a slip of paper with a word or phrase from the new vocabulary presented in Unit 10, such as *juku, kyōiku mama, kurabu katsudō, Nihon no gakkō no ichi nen, seifuku,* and *benkyō igai no koto.* Allow students five minutes to prepare a description of the item to present to the class. The other students then try to guess what is being described.

3. If you know someone who performs the Japanese tea ceremony, invite him or her to come to your class to give a demonstration.

Unit 11

Ask students to describe roles within their own family—for example, who cooks, cleans, holds a job, raises children, and so on. Have them compare these roles with those of the members of the Yamashita family.

Unit 12

1. Sing the Japanese New Year song, "Oshōgatsu" on page 175 with your class.

2. Ask students how they and their families celebrate the New Year. Ask them to make comparisons with the Japanese celebration.

Unit 13

Show pictures of Shinto shrines and Buddhist temples to familiarize students with roof styles, structures, altars, and other characteristics.

Unit 14

1. Wear a kimono to class, or invite a Japanese friend to model a kimono and demonstrate how it is worn.

2. If you can borrow several kimono, ask for student volunteers to model them and hold a "fashion show."

Unit 15

1. Show students *nengajō* you have received from Japan.

2. Show students how to write a simple New Year's greeting on a *nengajō*. Provide materials—paper, brushes, ink, writing samples—so that they can prepare greetings to send to the school principal, a favorite teacher, a guidance counselor, or a family member.

3. Bring Japanese New Year games such as *hanetsuki, koma, karuta, kendama,* or *daruma-otoshi* to class and teach the students how to play them.

Unit 16

1. If there are fruit trees in bloom in your area, picnic beneath them with your students as many Japanese do during cherry blossom season. Have the class write poems or haiku about the trees.

2. Teach your class the song "Sakura" on page 176.

Unit 17

Assign students to write a brief description in Japanese of their recollections of beginning school.

Unit 18

Ask students to imagine they are in Japan as exchange students. Have them write a letter home to their parents, relating two or three specific things they have learned about Japanese culture while living in Japan, such as the custom of wearing bathroom slippers.

Unit 19

1. Divide students into pairs to practice offering and accepting food the way Mrs. Ōshima and Mrs. Yamashita do in the story.

2. Ask class members how they might respond in Amy's situation. Would they tell Mrs. Ōshima that they were hungry and wanted something to eat?

Unit 20

Ask students to describe the one experience they think Amy will remember years after her visit to Japan is over.

RESOURCES FOR TEACHING ABOUT JAPAN

There are many resources that can greatly enrich the cultural aspects of *A Homestay in Japan.* The following bibliographies list sources for slides, videos, movies, books, and maps as well as some suggestions for teaching approaches and activities:

Fred Czarra. T*he Japan Database.* 1986. For purchasing information write to the Japan Database Project, Council of Chief State School Officers, 379 Hall of the States, 400 North Capitol Street N.W., Washington, D.C. 20001.

Nihongo Kyōzai Risuto: Guide to Japanese Language Teaching Materials. Bonjinsha Company, JAC Building, 5-5-35 Kōnan, Minato-ku, Tokyo 108, Japan. Annotated list of materials available through Bonjinsha. In English or Japanese.

Mutsuko Endo Simon. *A Practical Guide for Teachers of Elementary Japanese.* 1984. Center for Japanese Studies, University of Michigan, 108 Lane Hall, Ann Arbor, MI 48109.

Pictures illustrating everyday life in Japan can be invaluable teaching aids. Among possible sources are magazines such as *Japan Pictorial, Japan Echo, The East,* and *Look Japan,* and the book *A Day in the Life of Japan* (Toronto: Collins Publishers, 1985). Some audio-visual departments may be able to make slides from photographs in magazines and books, as long as fair use guidelines for educational copyright are followed.

Discover Japan: Words, Customs, and Concepts, Volumes 1 and 2 (Tokyo and New York: Kodansha International, 1982), previously published under the title *A Hundred Things Japanese,* is a good source of additional information on topics that are introduced in the culture notes.

The pamphlet "Facts and Figures of Japan" contains information for discussion topics, such as comparisons of how Japanese and American high school students spend their time. "What I Want to Know about Japan" provides basic information on such topics as climate and diet in Japan. Both pamphlets, as well as other materials, are available from the Japan Information Center, Consulate General of Japan, 299 Park Avenue, New York, NY 10171. The International Society for Educational Information (ISEI) publishes useful booklets such as "The Life of a Senior High School Student." These booklets may be obtained from ISEI, Kōryō Building, 18 Wakaba 1-chōme, Shinjuku-ku, Tokyo 160, Japan.

One source for classroom activities relating to Japan and Japanese culture is *Tanoshii Gakushū—Learning with Enjoyment,* by Michele Shoresman and Waunita Kinoshita, published by The Center for East Asian and Pacific Studies, University of Illinois, International Studies Building, 910 South 5th Street, Room 230, Champaign, IL 61820.

The New England Program for Teaching About Japan publishes a "Japan Resource Catalogue," which contains a comprehensive list of slide sets on topics such as the arts, daily life, and work and religion in Japan. The New England Program is one of several regional outreach programs throughout the United States that publish bibliographies and teaching materials about Japan. A complete list may be obtained from the National Precollegiate Japan Projects Network, 3104 Benjamin Building, College of Education, University of Maryland, College Park, MD 20742.

KANJI LIST

Following are the more than 450 kanji introduced in the Reader, unit by unit in order of appearance. Teachers can use this list as a guide when preparing supplementary materials for teaching writing. All students should be familiar with hiragana and katakana before beginning work on Unit 1.

Unit 1

出、会、日、本、着、三、間、四、
目、交、換、留、学、生、初、九、
月、一、何、度、汗、仲、少、心、
配、人、先、山、下、家、紹、介、
後、自、分、夫、婦、父、母、呼、
言、来、子、供、時、思、興、味、
持、私、焼、物、買、帰、知、喜、
話、全、部、大、国、教、今、所、
食、事、行、願

Unit 2

屋、族、別、車、店、入、向、数、
達、作、実、粉、方、冷、明、運、
取、使、回、上、手、落、笑、赤、
練、習、勉、強、音、立、気、郎、
表、説、心、中、見

Unit 3

連、門、玄、関、根、伝、統、的、
靴、脱、他、荷、年、分、二、階、
案、内、段、急、床、花、洋、服、
押、小、特、用、意、式

Unit 4

居、製、冊、品、英、語、書、包、
開、礼、座、遊、両、親、兄、弟、
聞、答、太、眠、長、風、呂、流、
横、虫、声、遠、浮、顔、元、好

Unit 5

朝、次、曜、起、考、洗、忘、台、
集、早、和、魚、最、前、茶、皿、
空、黄、色、形、切、計、画、話、
電、乗、番、商、街

Unit 6

紙、週、過、向、活、楽、町、道、
路、多、歩、外、近、寄、覚、当、
地、駅、水、同、違、口、制、女、
員、具、器、美、術、展、示、場、
世、界、料、試

Unit 7

毎、側、並、八、百、果、肉、住、
客、名、友、妻、位、決、絡、使、
以、感、慣、待

Unit 8

例、暑、飯、深、足、緒、失、湯、
船、叫、熱、終、細、仕、通

Unit 9

木、底、鉄、火、温、材、身、銭、
昔、男、払、衣、富、士、絵、描、
夕、涼、必、要

Unit 10

校、五、徒、史、理、写、真、動、
末、土、午、広、六、宿、題、晩、
高、育、葉、映、続、困、残、寒、
油、迷

Unit 11

夜、遅、十、夢、寝、社、飲、置、軽

Unit 12

正、相、談、休、福、神、貼、重、
箱、寿、司、歌、鏡、寺、除、鐘、
鳴、災、除、紅、白、合、戦

Unit 13

衣、勤、甘、酒、配、始、由、列、
丸、太、澄、打、歓、抱、者

Unit 14

卓、互、助

Unit 15

詣、駐、波、鳥、清、産、売、満、
順、建、様、鈴、済、賀、状

Unit 16

冬、春、桜、京、都、庭、然、濯、
干、破、送、祝、筆、文、房

Unit 17

青、晴、散、組、室、田、級、廊、
館、席、科

Unit 18

梅、雨、敗、突、傘、細、束、差、
贈、仏、恥、傷、化、直、島、返

Unit 19

翌、修、遠、慮、戻、注、申、訳、
若、発、便、利、布、団

Unit 20

招、解、辞、欲、造、窓、細、港、
悲、溶、込、飛、機、泣

A Homestay in Japan

TO THE STUDENT

Welcome to *A Homestay in Japan*. You may notice that this book looks quite different from the typical textbook that helps you learn the basic grammatical structures of a language. As the main title suggests, this book tells a story . . . a story about Amy, an American exchange student who lives for a year in Kobe with a Japanese host family, the Yamashitas. (The subtitle *Nihon to no Deai* appropriately means "An Encounter with Japan.") Mr. Yamashita is a businessman and his wife is a homemaker. They have a sixteen-year-old son, Ichirō, and two daughters—Akiko who is fourteen and Mayumi who is five.

Amy's story is divided into twenty units. In each unit you will find a reading section, an illustration, vocabulary lists, study questions and Culture Notes. A few songs and recipes are in the Appendixes.

Although all characters and events in the story are fictional, they are based on real people, events, and places. Caron Allen, one of the authors, went to Japan as an exchange student and lived there with a wonderful host family. While in Japan, Caron kept a diary about her experiences. Her diary provided the basis for much of this book. Caron's purpose in going to Japan was to study Japanese language and culture, in particular traditional music, art, architecture, and gardens. And indeed, that's what she did. But she found in Japan a great deal more, and this is what we have tried to capture for you in this book: enduring friendships; the warmth, kindness, and generosity of the people; and the rich texture of Japanese daily life. While *A Homestay in Japan* presents only a glimpse of Japanese culture, we hope that it will stimulate your curiosity and encourage you to explore Japanese life in deeper ways.

We hope that this book will also help you develop and strengthen your language skills and that you'll learn more about how Japanese is used in daily life. In the written texts you should be able to recognize many grammatical structures and vocabulary words that you learned in your first two or three years of language instruction. The level of difficulty stays fairly constant throughout the book, but we believe that as you learn techniques for reading Japanese, it may actually seem easier as you go along.

Most kanji when you first encounter them in our book are written with furigana—that is, the hiragana reading is printed above the kanji. Only the most basic kanji such as the kanji for *Nihon, iku,* and *kuru* are not written this way. We have also provided you with furigana readings whenever a familiar kanji appears in a new compound. The meanings for all new words and kanji are presented in the vocabulary lists. These definitions are also gathered at the back of the book in a complete glossary.

As you read through the book, you will notice that conversational Japanese is used whenever the characters are talking directly to each other. Elsewhere, you will notice the narrative style, where the "dictionary" or "plain" form of the verb is used. As family members and friends speak and interact with Amy, you will be able to see how speech styles vary according to the gender, age, and social relationship of the speakers. Although there are many regional dialects in Japan, we thought it best to stay with standard Japanese, rather than incorporate the local language spoken in the Kobe area. As a final note, we'd like to mention that although Amy is an American and new to Japanese culture, she speaks Japanese like a native. We know that this is not very realistic, but we felt that this approach was necessary in order to help our readers develop good language skills.

We hope that you will enjoy reading *A Homestay in Japan* and that you will use it as a starting point for pursuing your own interest in Japanese culture. Remember that you don't have to understand every word or every detail as you read. Just pick up as much as you can, and the rest will come later as your abilities grow. You may find that you don't always agree with Amy's responses to her new life in Japan. We hope that you will ask yourself what you might do in her situation and that some day you too will have the opportunity to experience Japan.

Caron Allen
Natsumi Watanabe

日本に着く

日本に着いてすぐ三日間のオリエンテーション
があった。四日目にパーティーがあった。そのパ
ーティーで、エイミーたち交換留学生は初めてホ
ストファミリーに会った。その日は九月一日で、
とてもむしあつい日だった。エイミーはハンカチ
で、何度も汗をふいた。ホストファミリーの人た
ちと仲よくできるかどうか少し心配だった。

やっとホストファミリーの人たちがやってき
た。先生がエイミーを山下さん一家に紹介した。
あいさつの後で、山下さんはエイミーに自分たち

出会い　an encounter, a meeting
着く　to arrive
三日間　three days
オリエンテーション　orientation
四日目　the fourth day
交換留学生　exchange student
初めて　for the first time
ホストファミリー　host family
むしあつい　hot and humid
ハンカチ　handkerchief*

何度も　many times, cf. 何人も
汗　sweat
仲よくできる，仲よくする　to get along
　well with
～かどうか　whether or not～
心配する　to worry
やっと　at last
やって来る　to come
一家　a household, a family
紹介する　to introduce

* = refer to the Culture Notes

夫婦のことをお父さん、お母さんと呼んでほしい
と言った。

エ：「やっと日本へ来ることができて、とても
うれしいです。日本には、子供の時からずっと来
てみたいと思っていました。」

父：「子供の時から。どうして日本に興味を
持ったんですか。」

エ：「そうですね。私が子供のころ、父が日本
に来た時、焼き物や着物なんかを買って帰ったん
です。それがとてもきれいで。それからは、ただ
もう日本のことが知りたくて。」

子供：「そして私たちは、アメリカのことが
もっと知りたいのよね。」

父：「そうだね。」

エ：「私の家のことなら喜んで話しますけど、

夫婦　husband and wife
呼んでほしい／てほしい＝てもらいたい
〜ことができる　can, be able to〜
興味　an interest

焼き物　pottery
ただもう　emphasizes 知りたい
なら　if〜, then〜
喜ぶ　to be happy

アメリカのことを全部はちょっと... とても大き

い国ですから。」

　父：「日本のことについてなら、いろいろなこ

とを教えてあげたいと思っているんですよ。まず

今日は、ちょっとおもしろい所で食事をしようと

思っているのですが行きますか。」

_There are various
things about JJ
want to teach.
Shall we go to
dinner._

～（に）ついて　regarding～　　　　食事をする　to have dinner (a meal)

第一課　練習問題
<small>だいいっか　れんしゅうもんだい</small>

I. A. 質問に答えなさい
<small>しつもん　こた</small>

1. オリエンテーションは何日間でしたか。
2. パーティーは何月何日にありましたか。あつかったですか。 *Sept. 1st humid*
3. エィミーのホストファミリーは何という名前ですか。 *ちちてはは*
4. エィミーはいつごろから日本に来てみたいと思っていましたか。
5. エィミーはどうして日本に興味を持っていましたか。 *Dad brought back cool*
6. 山下さんの子供たちは何のことを知りたがっていますか。

B. True or False

1. エィミーが日本に着いてすぐ四日目にパーティーがありました。
2. エィミーはパーティーで先生に会いました。
3. エィミーの子供の時、エィミーの父が日本に来ました。
4. エィミーはアメリカのことなら、何でも知っています。
5. パーティーの後で、みんなは食事をしました。

II. つぎの質問に答えなさい

1. あなたは日本に興味を持っていますか。それはどうしてですか。
2. あなたは日本のことを勉強していますか。それはどんなことですか。
3. あなたは日本人にアメリカのことがせつめいできますか。たとえば、どんなことですか。

第一課　Unit 1
練習　to practice
問題　question(s), problem(s)

質問　question(s)
答える　to answer

—————— Unit 1 Culture Notes ——————

Speech Levels

The level of politeness in the Japanese language most often indicates the degree of respect, formality, and social distance between speakers. For example, within the intimate "inside" group of the family, plain forms of speech are most often used. The family unit as a whole is regarded as being greater than any one individual, so status distinctions between family members are not as pronounced as those between two strangers.

Between strangers, there is greater psychological and emotional distance. Honorific forms are used, especially for introductions and formal social situations such as business meetings or weddings.

hankachi

The Japanese most often use handkerchiefs to keep their faces dry and comfortable during hot weather, and not to blow their nose.

第二課 UNIT 2

そば屋へ

　エィミーと山下さん一家はほかの留学生や家族、そして先生と別れて，車でそば屋に行った。のれんをくぐって、店に入った。カウンターの向こうがわでは、数人の人がいそがしそうにしていた。

　エ：「お父さん、あの人達は何をしているんですか。」

　父：「おそばを作っているんですよ。」

　エ：「おそばって何ですか。」

　父：「そばの実から作った粉でできているめんですよ。そばにはいろいろな食べ方があります。

そば　buckwheat noodles
そば屋　a noodle restaurant*
〜（と）別れる　to part from
のれん　a shop curtain*
くぐる　to pass through, under
カウンター　counter (architectural structure)

向こうがわ　the other side
数人　several people, a few persons
実　a seed
粉　flour
めん（めんるい）　noodles
〜方　a manner, a way, how to〜

今日はあついから、冷たいそばにしようと思いま
す。いいですか。」

エ：「ええ。冷たいのはどうやって食べるんで
すか。」

父：「こい目のつゆに、きざみねぎやおろした
しょうがを入れて、それにそばをつけて食べるん
ですよ。」

明子：「おいしいのよ。食べてみて。」

ウェートレスがそばを運んできた。エィミーは
フォークをさがしたが、はししかなかった。おず
おずと、エィミーははしを取った。

母：「エィミーさんはおはしが使えるんです
か。」

_____

冷たい　cold (not applicable to the weather)
こい目　strong (as in taste or flavor)
つゆ　soup, broth
きざむ　to mince
ねぎ　green onion
おろす　to grate
しょうが　ginger

つける　to dip
〜てみる　to try
運ぶ　to carry
さがす　to look for
〜しかない　there is only〜
おずおず（と）　hesitantly, nervously

エ：「何回か使ったことがあります。でもあま

り上手じゃありません。」　エィミーはそばをは

しでつまんだが、ひざの上に落としてしまった。

家族のみんなが笑ったので、エィミーは赤くなっ

た。

お母さんがやさしく言った。

母：「かまいませんよ、エィミーさん。おそば

をおはしで食べるのはとてもむずかしいんです。

でもちょっと練習すれば上手になりますよ。がん

ばってくださいね。」

エ：「ええ、がんばります。日本のことをたく

さん勉強しなくちゃなりませんね。」

明子がエィミーにそばを食べてみせた。エィミ

ーもやってみた。今度はうまくいった。

～たことがある　with a past tense verb = have had the experience of～	落とす　to drop (something)
	笑う　to laugh
つまむ　to hold between (in this case, chopsticks)	かまいません　it's o.k., it's all right
	練習する　to practice
すべる　to slide, be slippery	すれば、えば　if (in this context)
ぬりばし　lacquered chopsticks	うまくいく　to go well
ひざ　lap	

[handwritten margin notes: "Couldn't think of anything but slurping sound", "Don't make sound but it's ok cause shows u like it", "A little embarrassed her american mom wouldn't like that"]

エィミーは家族がズルズルと、音を立てて食べるのが気になった。「アメリカでは、食べる時にそんなに音を立てないんですけど。」とエィミーは言った。一郎が「日本では、そばを食べる時に音を立てるのはおいしさを表すためで、かまわないことなんだよ。」と説明した。「そうなんですか。じゃ、私も音を立ててみます。」とエィミーは言った。

エィミーも音を立てて食べてみた。やはりちょっとはずかしかった。心の中でアメリカのお母さんに見つかったら、しかられるだろうな、と思った。

ズルズルと音を立てて食べる　to make a slurping sound while eating
気になる　to get (something) into one's head to the point where one can't think of anything else
表す　to show

かまわないこと　an acceptable thing
（かまう＝ to mind, to care about, to be concerned about）
説明する　to explain
はずかしい　embarrassed, shy
見つかる　to be found out
しかる　to scold

━━━━ 第二課　練習問題 ━━━━

I.　A.　質問に答えなさい

　　1.　エィミーと山下さん一家は何でそば屋に行きましたか。

　　2.　カウンターでは、数人の人が何をしていましたか。

　　3.　そばとは何ですか。

　　4.　エィミーははしが使えますか。

　　5.　そばを食べる時にどうして音を立てても
　　　　かまわないのですか。

　　B.　True or False

　　1.　エィミーと山下さん一家は先生とそば屋に行きました。

　　2.　みんなは冷たいそばを食べました。

　　3.　そばには一つしか食べ方がありません。

　　4.　一郎がエィミーにそばを食べてみせました。

　　5.　日本では、そばを食べる時に音を立てるのは
　　　　めずらしいです。

II.　つぎの質問に答えなさい

　　1.　そばを食べたことがありますか。それはいつですか。

　　2.　日本の食べ物が好きですか。たとえば、どんな食べ物
　　　　ですか。

—— Unit 2 Culture Notes ——

sobaya

The noodle shop mentioned in this unit happens to make and serve its own noodles, as do many noodle shops in Japan. Some shops serve pre-packaged noodles, and many offer different varieties of noodles.

noren

A *noren* is a short curtain hung at the top of a doorway in shops, restaurants, and public baths. Printed words and designs indicate the name and type of business. *Noren* can also be hung in the kitchen and hall doorways of private homes.

第三課 UNIT 3　山下さんの家へ

　山下さん一家はエィミーを家に連れていった。みんなは門をくぐって、玄関に着いた。その家はかわら屋根の伝統的な日本の家だった。

　玄関で、エィミーが靴を脱いでいる間に、他の人はスリッパにはきかえた。お母さんがエィミーにもスリッパをくれた。「それがエィミーさんのスリッパよ。」とよこから明子が言った。エィミーは四つのスーツケースを持ってきていた。そのうちの一つはおみやげでいっぱいだった。

　母：「ほんとうにたくさんお荷物を持ってきたんですね。」

くぐる → pass through.

連れる　to take with
門　gate
✴玄関　an entranceway*
　かわら　tile (for the roof)
✴屋根　a roof
✴伝統的　traditional,　伝統＝ tradition
　靴　shoes
✴脱ぐ　to take off

間（に）　while
スリッパ　slippers
はきかえる　to change into,
　　cf. 靴をはく、靴を脱ぐ
スーツケース　suitcase
✴（お）みやげ　souvenir*
　荷物　baggage

エ：「一年分（いちねんぶん）ですもの。」

明子がエィミーを二階（にかい）の部屋（へや）に案内（あんない）してくれた。階段（かいだん）がとても急（きゅう）だったので、エィミーはこわくなった。お父さんがエィミーの後（うし）ろから荷物（にもつ）を運（はこ）んでくれた。部屋（へや）はきれいな日本間（にほんま）だった。床（とこ）の間（ま）にはかけじくがかかっていた。エィミーのためにきれいな生（い）け花（ばな）も生（い）けてあった。明子がエィミーにつくえと洋服（ようふく）だんすを見せてくれた。

エ：「ベッドはどこですか。」

明子：「押（お）し入（い）れの中よ。」

エ：「ええっ。ベッドを押（お）し入（い）れの中に入（い）れてあるんですか。」

〜もの　because
二階　second floor　にかい
部屋　room　へや
案内する　to show around　あんない
階段　stairs, staircase*　かいだん
急（な）　steep
日本間　a Japanese-style room*　cf. 洋間
床の間　an alcove for the display of art*
かけじく　a hanging scroll, cf. かけもの
かかる　to hang

生け花　flower arrangement*
生ける　to arrange (flowers and such) in a vase
〜てある　has been〜, is〜
つくえ　desk
洋服だんす　a wardrobe　（洋服＝western-style clothes）　ようふくだんす
ベッド　bed
押し入れ　a closet used mainly for the storage of futon　おしいれ

明子：「ベッドじゃなくて、おふとんなんです
よ。見せましょうか。」

明子は押し入れからふとんを取り出して、しい
て見せてくれた。エィミーはねっしんにそれを見
ていた。

エ：「わあ、何てきれいなもようでしょう。そ
れにフカフカですね。気持ちがよさそうだわ。で
も、ずいぶん小さいまくらですね。こんなに小さ
いまくら、見たことがありません。あら、このま
くら、音がするわ。何が入っているんですか。」

明子：「あずきですよ。」

エ：「あずきですって。」

明子：「ええ。そばがらを入れることもありま
すよ。エィミーさんのために特別に用意したんで

ふとん　Japanese-style bedding
米取り出す　to take out
しく　to spread out, to lay (something) down
米ねっしん（に）　eagerly
何て（きれいなもよう）　what a (pretty
　design)
もよう　design, pattern

米フカフカ　soft, fluffy
米まくら　pillow
あずき　a kind of small red bean (adzuki)
そばがら　buckwheat hulls
米特別に　specially
米用意する　to prepare

すよ。私達が今使っているまくらはほとんどアメ

リカ式のなんですけど。」

　エ：「私のためにですか。まあ、どうもありが

とう。」

　明子：「どういたしまして。じゃ、下へ行きま

しょうか。」

_____

✳ほとんど　mainly, mostly
✳アメリカ式　American style, cf. 日本式，洋式

———— 第三課　練習問題 ————

I. A. 質問に答えなさい
　　1. 山下さんの家はどんな家ですか。
　　2. みんなはどこで靴を脱ぎましたか。何にはきかえましたか。
　　3. 一つのスーツケースの中は何でいっぱいでしたか。
　　4. エィミーはどうしてこわくなりましたか。
　　5. 押し入れの中に何がありましたか。
　　6. 日本式のベッドは何といいますか。

　　B. True or False
　　1. エィミーはスーツケースを一つ持ってきました。
　　2. エィミーの部屋は日本間です。
　　3. エィミーのまくらにはそばがらが入っています。
　　4. ほとんどのアメリカ式のまくらにはあずきが入っています。
　　5. ふとんはフカフカで気持ちよさそうです。

II. つぎの質問に答えなさい
　　ふとんを見たことがありますか。それはいつですか。
　　アメリカ式のベッドとはどう違いますか。

———— Unit 3 Culture Notes ————

genkan

The *genkan* is the entryway to the home where family members and guests remove their shoes and change into slippers. There is usually a cupboard for shoe storage and perhaps an umbrella stand. The main house is elevated one step above the level of the *genkan*.

omiyage

Gift-giving is a vital aspect of Japanese life. Visitors to Japan should always bring small gifts to their hosts. (See Unit 4 Culture Notes.)

kaidan

In order to conserve space, staircases in Japanese houses are often narrower and steeper than those found in many American homes.

Nihonma

Traditional Japanese-style rooms usually contain the following elements:

tatami

These woven straw mats are approximately two inches thick and six feet long by three feet wide. They cover all or part of a floor area in a variety of prescribed placement patterns.

tokonoma

The *tokonoma* is a special alcove with a raised platform and often a shelf or series of shelves. It is traditionally used for the display of art such as hanging scrolls, ceramics, and flower arrangements. Nowadays, due to lack of space, television sets are often placed in the *tokonoma*.

ikebana

Japanese flower arrangement is a highly developed art.

fusuma

These sliding doors consist of a wood frame covered on both sides with decorative paper or painted with nature scenes. *Fusuma* may be used to separate rooms or may be removed to combine rooms into larger spaces.

shōji

These windows or sliding doors are made of wooden lattices covered on one side with white paper. *Shōji* are most often used along the external walls of a home, such as corridor areas and windows.

A traditional Japanese-style room is multi-functional. Bedding is stored in closets by day so the room can be converted into a study, a dining room, or a playroom, according to the need at the time. In contrast, modern Japanese apartments and some houses have rooms with fixed walls, each room serving a particular function.

Hospitality

Guests receive special treatment in Japan. Since Amy is a foreigner and an exchange student, the Yamashitas assume that she is interested in traditional culture and want to offer her the opportunity to experience such things as adzuki pillows. Even though the Yamashitas and many other Japanese no longer use these pillows, Amy is offered this "old-fashioned" item as a courtesy. A typical American pillow would be offered as well.

Further Reading

For a comprehensive look at *ikebana*, consult Shozo Sato, *The Art of Arranging Flowers: A Complete Guide to Japanese Ikebana* (New York: Harry N. Abrams, 1966).

山下家で

エィミーと明子は居間におりていった。居間に

はカーペットがしいてあり、ソファー、いす、カ

ラーテレビなどがあった。エィミーはおみやげの

入ったスーツケースを居間に運んだ。その中には

お父さんのためのアメリカ製のウイスキー、お母

さんのための何冊かの本とアメリカのししゅう

用品、子供達のためのチョコレートと英語の書い

てあるティーシャツなどが入っていた。

みんながとてもていねいに包みを開くので、

エィミーはびっくりした。チョコレートを食べな

がらみんながお礼を言った。それまではずかし

居間　living room	用品　supplies
おりる　to go down, to descend	チョコレート　chocolate
カーペット　carpet	ティーシャツ　T-shirt
ソファー　sofa	ていねいに　carefully
いす　chair	包み　a package
～製　made in～	開く（ひらく）　to open
ウイスキー　whiskey	びっくりする　to be surprised
冊　a volume (a counter suffix for books)	（お）礼を言う　to express thanks
ししゅう　embroidery	それまで　until then

がっていたまゆみがエィミーのところに来て、ひざに座った。エィミーはうれしくなってまゆみと遊んであげた。

お母さんが日本のおかしを運んできた。エィミーは初めておまんじゅうを食べた。それはとてもおいしかった。「おまんじゅうはおいしいし、おそばよりずっと食べやすいですね。」とエィミーは言った。

エィミーはみんなにアメリカの両親のしゃしんを見せた。エィミーには兄弟がない。お母さんが「さびしくなりませんか。」と聞いたので、エィミーは「ええ、時々さびしくなりますね。」と答えた。少し太っているエィミーの父を見て、一郎が「アメリカ人はみんな大きいんですね。」と言った。エィミーは笑って「そうですね。」と答えた。

～がる　looks like～, shows signs of～
座る　to sit
うれしい　happy
おかし　sweet(s)
（お）まんじゅう　a bun with bean jam
　　filling（one type of Japanese sweet）

両親　parents
兄弟　sibling(s)
さびしい　lonely
答える　to answer
太っている　to be fat

明子とまゆみはもう眠そうだった。エィミーも長い一日の後でとてもつかれていた。明子が日本の風呂の入り方を教えてくれた。一日の汗を流した後で、急な階段をのぼり、部屋のふすまを開けた。エィミーはたおれるように横になった。

今まで聞いたこともないふしぎな虫の声を聞いていると、むねがいっぱいになってなみだが出てきた。私はどこにいるんだろう、何をしているんだろう、なんで遠い所へ来てしまったんだろう...いろいろな思いが浮かんだ。でも、ホストファミリーの人達のやさしい顔を思い出すと元気が出てきた。「きっと日本が好きになるわ。」とエィミーは思った。

眠い　sleepy（眠る　to sleep）
つかれている　to be tired
風呂　a bath
風呂に入る　to take a bath
流す　to wash off
開ける　to open
たおれる　to collapse, to fall
横になる　to lie (down)
ふしぎ（な）　strange, mysterious
虫　insect
声　a voice, (a call of an insect)
むね　the chest

むねがいっぱいになる　(one's) chest becomes filled with emotion
なみだ　tears
思い　a thought
浮かぶ　to float
思いが浮かぶ　thoughts come across one's mind
やさしい　soft, gentle
顔　a face
思い出す　to remember
元気が出てくる　to cheer up
きっと　surely

第四課　練習問題

I. A. 質問に答えなさい
1. 山下さんの家の居間には何がありましたか。
2. エィミーのスーツケースの中にはどんな物が入っていましたか。
3. どうしてエィミーはうれしかったのですか。
4. エィミーはみんなにだれのしゃしんを見せましたか。
5. だれがエィミーに日本の風呂の入り方を教えてくれましたか。
6. エィミーはふしぎな虫の声を聞いてどうなりましたか。

B. True or False
1. みんながまんじゅうを食べながらお礼を言いました。
2. みんながとてもていねいに包みを開きました。
3. エィミーは初めてまんじゅうを食べました。
4. エィミーには兄弟がいます。
5. 一郎はアメリカ人はみんな大きいと思っています。

II. 次の質問に答えなさい
1. もし日本へ行くとしたら、どんなおみやげを持っていきますか。
2. あなたの家の居間にはどんな物がありますか。

—————— Unit 4 Culture Notes ——————

Gift-giving

Gift-giving is an important part of social interaction in Japan. The complex guidelines that govern gift exchanges vary according to the occasion and the relative status of the people involved. In fact, etiquette guides are now available to those who are uncertain about the appropriate manner of exchange.

Major events for gift-giving include birth, coming of age, marriage, death, illness, and parting. Gifts are usually given to the whole family rather than to an individual. Great care is taken to select a gift of correct value.

Gifts (*temiyage*) can also be presented simply on the occasion of a visit to a friend's home. Souvenirs, or *omiyage*, are given to family and friends even if the giver has only taken a one-day excursion.

There are two major seasons for gift-giving. One, called *ochūgen*, occurs around mid-year. The other occurs at year's end, and is called *oseibo*. Gifts given at these two times carry with them a sense of obligation and social duty and are thus presented to superiors—employers, teachers, or those to whom one is indebted. No return gifts are required because the gifts are already a return for patronage or a favor received. About one month prior to each gift-giving season, department stores set up displays of prepackaged gift items and make their employees available to assist customers in selecting a gift. Gifts can be ordered and delivered directly to the recipient's home.

One of the most popular and traditional gift items is food, but during *ochūgen* and *oseibo*, many other items such as household goods are given as well. Children are given gifts of money (*otoshidama*) on New Year's Day.

If the exchange of gifts is a complicated matter, so is the wrapping and presentation. A visitor to Japan will marvel at the style, variety, and elegance of Japanese packaging and gift-wrapping. Different colors and styles of packaging are used for different occasions. For formal, happy occasions, white paper is used. The package is bound with a special red and white tie called a *mizuhiki*. For weddings, the *mizuhiki* is often silver and gold. Nowadays it is common to see the image of the *mizuhiki* imprinted directly onto the paper. For somber occasions such as funerals, the *mizuhiki* is gray and white or black and white. When money is presented as a gift, the notes are always crisp and clean and placed in a special envelope, often decorated with a *mizuhiki*.

Gifts are presented to teachers of traditional arts by their students when first beginning lessons as an advance offering of thanks. Amy brought gifts to her family as a way of thanking them for the help she would receive throughout the year.

Further Reading

Kunio Ekiguchi. *Gift Wrapping: Creative Ideas from Japan.* Tokyo and New York: Kodansha International, 1985.

Hideyuki Oka. *How to Wrap Five Eggs.* New York: Harper and Row, 1967.

———. *How to Wrap Five More Eggs.* New York: Weatherhill, 1975.

朝ごはん
（あさ）

次の日は日曜日だった。お母さんと明子が朝食

の用意をした。お母さんが階段の下に来て「エィ

ミーさん、一郎、ごはんですよ。」と大声で呼ん

だ。明子はまゆみを起こしに行った。まゆみはま

だ両親のふとんの中で眠っていた。

エィミーは起きて二階のトイレに行った。その

トイレは洋式でとても小さかった。ドアを開ける

とスリッパがあった。「いったいどうしてここに

スリッパがあるのかしら。」と考えながらエィミ

ーはそこに立っていた。するとあくびをしながら

一郎がやってきた。

朝　morning	洋式　western style
ごはん　a meal	ドア　door
次の　next	いったい　how on earth!
朝食　breakfast	考える　to think
大声で　in a loud voice	立つ　to stand
起こす　to wake (someone) up	すると　just then
起きる　to get up out of bed	あくびする　to yawn
トイレ　toilet*	

一郎：「どうかしたの。」

エ：「いえ、あの、だれかお手洗いにスリッパ

を忘れたんでしょうか。」

一郎：（笑いながら）「そうじゃないんだよ。

これはトイレ用なのさ。トイレに入る時は、それ

まではいていたスリッパを脱いで、これにはきか

えるんだよ。」

「そうなんですか。」とエィミーは言ったがど

うしてそうするのかよくわからなかった。

家族は台所に集まって「お早う。」、「お早う

ございます。」とおたがいに朝のあいさつをして

いた。

父：「よく眠れましたか、エィミーさん。」

エ：「ええ、とても。」

どうかしたの is there anything wrong? cf.どうしたの what's wrong?	さ indeed, you know (sentence-ending particle)
忘れる to forget (in this context, "to leave behind")	はく to put on, to wear (shoes)
～用 use of～	台所 kitchen
	集まる to gather
	（お）たがいに with each other, mutually

母：「和風のごはんでいいかしら。」

エ：「ええ、何ですか。」

母：「ごはんとおみそしる、おつけ物と焼き魚

ですよ。」

お母さんが最初にエイミーにごはんを出してく

れた。エイミーの前にはごはん用の茶わん、みそ

しる用のぬりわん、魚の皿、それに小さい空の皿

があった。明子が黄色いつけ物を小さい皿に入れ

てくれた。

エ：「おつけ物ですって。アメリカのおつけ物

はたいていみどり色なんですが．．．」

明：「これはたくあんというのよ。日本のつけ

和風　Japanese style	皿　plate, dish
みそしる　miso soup	それに　besides, and also
つけ物　pickles	空　empty
焼き魚　broiled fish	黄色い　yellow
最初に　first	色　color
ごはん　rice (in this context, can also mean "a meal")	大てい　usually
茶わん　a rice bowl	みどり色　green
ぬりわん　a lacquered bowl	たくあん　pickled daikon (radish)

物は形も色も大きさも色々あるの。一切れ食べて
みて。おいしいのよ。」

　食事中みんなはその日の計画をエィミーに話し
た。まず明子が電車の乗り方を教えて、二人で明
子の一番好きなデパートへ買い物に行く。次にお
母さんと三人で商店街へ買い物に行くのだそう
だ。みんながゆっくり食事をしている間に、エィ
ミーはその日の用意をした。

形　shape　かたち
大きさ　size　おおきさ
色々　various　いろいろ
一切れ　a slice　ひときで
食事中　during a meal　ちゅうくじ ちゅう
計画　a plan　けいかく

乗る　to get on　のる
デパート　department store
買い物に行く　to go shopping　かいもの に行く
次に　afterwards, after that　つぎに
商店街　a shop-lined street, a shopping district
　しょうてんがい

—— 第五課　練習問題 ——

I.　A. 質問に答えなさい
　　1. だれが朝食の用意をしましたか。
　　2. まゆみはどこで眠っていましたか。　両親のふとんの中
　　3. エィミーは起きてからどこに行きましたか。　にかいのトイレ
　　4. 二階のトイレのドアを開けると何がありましたか。
　　　 それはどうしてですか。
　　5. 食事中みんなはどんなことを話しましたか。

　　B. True or False
　　1. 二階のトイレは日本式でした。　F
　　2. 家族は台所に集まりました。
　　3. エィミーはよく眠れませんでした。
　　4. 日本のつけ物は形も色も大きさも色々あります。
　　5. エィミーはその日の計画を家族に話しました。　F

II. 次の質問に答えなさい
　　1. 和風の朝食はあなたの毎日の朝食とどう違いますか。
　　2. 日本のつけ物を食べたことがありますか。
　　　 どんなつけ物でしたか。好きですか。
　　3. 日本へ行ったら和食を食べてみたいですか。どうしてですか。

—— Unit 5 Culture Notes ——

toire	A *toire* is a small room containing only a toilet fixture; it does not include a bathtub. The toilet can be either American-style or Japanese-style (a floor fixture over which a person squats).
surippā	In addition to bathroom slippers, house slippers are worn in the hallways and in rooms which are not covered with *tatami.*
Mayumi wa . . . nemutteita	It is not unusual for infants and small children to sleep in the same room as their parents.
Japanese Cuisine	The preparation and presentation of food is considered an art in Japan. Colors, shapes, and textures are combined for taste as well as for visual appeal. Freshness is emphasized. Since nothing is overcooked or heavily seasoned, food retains its color and natural flavor. Food and dishes are coordinated and matched according to the season. For example, because bamboo or glass dishes convey a cool, fresh feeling they will most often be used in the summer.
	Small amounts of different foods are served on separate dishes. The artistic arrangement is meant to be food for the soul, making the meal more appetizing and inspiring a certain appreciation and thanksgiving for the food.

Further Reading

Elizabeth Andoh. *At Home with Japanese Cooking*. New York: Alfred A. Knopf, 1980.

Yukiko and Bob Haydock. *Japanese Garnishes: The Ancient Art of Mukimono*. New York: Holt, Rinehart and Winston, 1980.

Kinjiro Omae and Yuzuru Tachibana. *The Book of Sushi*. Tokyo and New York: Kodansha International, 1981.

Angela Terzani. *Japan: The Beauty of Food*. New York: Rizzoli, 1987.

Yoshio Tsuchiya. *A Feast for the Eyes: The Japanese Art of Food Arrangement*. Tokyo and New York: Kodansha International, 1985.

Shizuo Tsuji. *Japanese Cooking: A Simple Art*. Tokyo and New York: Kodansha International, 1980.

James Udesky. *The Book of Soba*. Tokyo and New York: Kodansha International, 1988.

手紙を書く　その一

　数週間が過ぎた。その間とても忙しくて、エィ
ミーは両親にみじかい手紙しか出していなかっ
た。やっと時間ができたので、エィミーは長い手
紙を書くことにした。エィミーはざぶとんを出し
て机に向かった。まどの外のかわらの屋根をなが
めながら、どうやって両親に日本の生活を説明し
ようかと考えた。

　　お父さん、お母さん

　　お元気ですか。私は元気です。日本の生活
　はとても楽しく、山下さん一家はとても親切
　です。いつか会ってほしいと思います。

数週間　several weeks
過ぎる　to pass
その間　during that time
忙しい　busy
手紙　a letter
出す　to send
〜ことにする　to decide to〜
ざぶとん　a floor cushion*

机に向かう　to sit at one's desk
まど　window
ながめる　to stare out (the window)
どうやって　how
生活　life
楽しい　enjoyable
親切　kind

日本の町はどこでも家がたくさんあります。道路はせまく、車と人が多いので、歩くのがたいへんなこともあります。

子供達は外国人を見るとこわがることがあります。でも近寄ってきて私にさわる子や後ろをついてくる子もいます。「ハロー」とか「外人」とか「ジャイアント」と言った子までいました。おもしろいけれどいやになることもあります。

お父さん、私が日本食を食べられるかどうか心配していたのを覚えていますか。日本食はおいしいですよ。それにとてもきれいです。ところでここにはアメリカのファースト

町　city, town
道路　road
せまい　narrow
多い　many
外国人　foreigner
こわがる　to fear
近寄る　to come near
さわる　to touch
後ろ　behind

ついてくる　to follow
ハロー　hello
外人　foreigner (colloquial for 外国人)*
ジャイアント　giant
日本食　Japanese cuisine, cf. 洋食
覚える　to remember
ところで　by the way
ファーストフード　fast food

フードのお店（みせ）もたくさんありますので、ハンバーガーがほしいと思ったら、いつでも買えますからご心配なく。

ええと、他にどんなおもしろいことがあるでしょうか。ああ、そうそう、お母さんは買い物が大好きだから日本の買い物について書きましょう。これは本当（ほんとう）にすごいですよ。先日（せんじつ）明子ちゃんが地下街（ちかがい）のショッピングセンターと駅（えき）のすぐ横の二つのデパートに連れていってくれました。

センターの中にはいろいろなお店（みせ）やレストランがあります。一番上の階には滝（たき）やふん水などもあってとてもきれいです。

ショッピングセンターを見た後、デパートに行きました。デパートには何でもありま

店　a store
ハンバーガー　a hamburger
ご心配なく　please don't worry
ええと　um, well
すごい　amazing
先日　the other day

地下街　an underground market
ショッピングセンター　a shopping center
横に　alongside, next to
滝　a waterfall
ふん水　fountain

す。一階はアメリカのデパートと同じよう
に、こう水、ネクタイなどがあります。違い
は入り口の所やエスカレーターの所に案内を
する制服を着た女の店員がいることです。

　他の階には家具、食器、おもちゃ、洋服、
日本の着物などがあります。その他に美術品
の展示会や屋上には子供の遊び場まであるの
です。でも何よりもすごいのは地下です。世
界中から集めた食料品があります。ただの試
食品があるので、私はアメリカのチョコレー
ト、中国のおまんじゅう、それにフランスの
おかしを食べました。お父さんもお母さんも
きっと好きになりますよ。

同じように　in the same way
　（同じ＝the same）
こう水　perfume
ネクタイ　necktie
違い　a difference
エスカレーター　escalator
制服　a uniform
店員　a clerk, a salesperson
家具　furniture
食器　tableware
おもちゃ　toy(s)

美術品の展示会　an art exhibition
　（美術＝ art)
屋上　a flat rooftop
遊び場　a play area
地下　basement （in this context)
世界中　all over the world
食料品　foodstuffs
ただ　free
試食品　sample food products
中国　China

第六課　練習問題

I. A. 質問に答えなさい
1. エィミーはだれに手紙を書きましたか。
2. エィミーは日本の生活をどう思っていますか。
3. 日本の道路は広いですか。
4. 日本の子供達は外国人を見るとどんなことをしますか。
5. エィミーと明子はどこへ買い物に行きましたか。
6. 日本のデパートには何がありますか。

B. True or False
1. エィミーは両親にみじかい手紙を書くことにしました。
2. 日本には家も車もたくさんあります。
3. エィミーは日本食がきらいです。
4. 日本にはアメリカのファーストフードの店があります。
5. 日本のデパートの地下には食料品は何でもあります。

II. 次の質問に答えなさい
日本のデパートに買い物へ行くとしたら、どんな物を買いますか。

Unit 6 Culture Notes

zabuton

A *zabuton* is a floor cushion. Amy's room is Japanese style; there are no chairs. Her desk is low to the floor, so she sits on a *zabuton*. The Yamashita children all have Western-style bedrooms. Many middle- and upper-class homes contain rooms of both styles.

gaijin

A foreigner in a large international city like Tokyo can remain anonymous. In smaller cities and rural areas where the presence of foreigners is less common, anyone who looks racially different is quite noticeable. Children are the least shy about expressing their surprise.

depāto

Department stores in Japan grew out of traditional dry goods businesses. They began to take on their present appearance in the early twentieth century. Private railway companies created their own department stores, situating them at major terminals. Today, many Japanese department stores feature lounges, restaurants, coffee shops, playgrounds for children, free delivery for most gift items, art exhibitions, and concerts.

第七課 UNIT 7 手紙を書く　その二

　　毎日の買い物には、家の近くの商店街へ行きます。商店街は小さい商店が道の両側にずっと並んでいる所で、その道には屋根がつけてあるので、モールみたいです。そこには八百屋や果物屋、肉屋、魚屋、パン屋、洋服屋、本屋などがあります。

　　お店の人はお店の二階や奥に住んでいるので、近所のお客さんの名前をみんな知っています。ですから、いつも友達の家で買い物しているような気持ちになります。すてきでしょう。

_____

商店　a shop, a store
道　a path, a street
両側（に）　(on) both sides, either side
並ぶ　to line (a street)
モール　mall
八百屋　a vegetable store
果物屋　a fruit store
肉屋　a meat shop
魚屋　a fish shop

パン屋　a bakery
本屋　a bookstore
奥　the innermost part of the first floor behind the public shop area
住む　to live in, to reside at
近所　neighborhood
（お）客さん　customer(s)
気持ち　a feeling

近くにはスーパーマーケットもあるので、山下さんのお母さんがそのうち連れて行ってくださるそうです。

お父さんもお母さんも知っているように、山下さんご夫妻は私のことをとても心配してくださっています。お父さんやお母さんよりもきびしい位です。家に帰る時間は決められているし、出かけている時もいつもどこにいるのか連絡しなければなりません。時々いやになりますが、山下さんの心配する気持ちもわかります。

私がさびしくないかと気を使って、他の交換留学生に電話をかけたくないかと聞いてくださいます。たとえ私がさびしくないと言っ

スーパーマーケット　a supermarket
そのうち　soon, before long
知っているように～　I'm quite sure
　　you know～
ご夫妻　Mr. and Mrs.
きびしい　strict
位　about, to the extent of

決める　to decide (on), to arrange
出かける　to go out
連絡する　to inform, to notify
いやになる　to become tired of, averse to
気を使う　to care about, to worry about
たとえ　although, even though

ても、二時間以上私を部屋の中に一人にして
おくことはありません。私がさびしいと感じ
るのは日本語や習慣がわからない時です。け
れど、こんな気持ちはすぐなくなります。元
気でやっていますから、ご心配なく。お手紙
を待っています。

エイミー

以上　more than
一人にしておく　to leave (someone) alone
感じる　to feel

習慣　custom
すぐなくなります　to go away quickly

―――― 第七課　練習問題 ――――

I. A. 質問に答えなさい
1. 「毎日の買い物」では、どんな物を買いますか。
2. 商店街にはどんな店がありますか。
3. 店の人はどこに住んでいますか。どうして友達の所で
　 買い物をしているような気持ちになりますか。
4. エィミーはどんな時さびしいと感じますか。
5. 山下さんのお父さんとお母さんはどういうふうにきびしいですか。

B. True or False
1. 家の近くには商店街があります。
2. 商店街の道には屋根がついています。
3. エィミーの両親は山下さんのお父さんとお母さんよりも
　 きびしいです。
4. 山下さんの家の近くにはスーパーマーケットがあります。
5. 山下夫妻はエィミーがさびしいかどうか気を使うことが
　 ありません。

II. 次の質問に答えなさい
あなたの両親はきびしいですか。説明しなさい。

—— Unit 7 Culture Notes ——

Grocery Stores

Some groceries in major cities resemble American-style supermarkets with fairly wide aisles and lots of packaged foods. Smaller neighborhood groceries—in addition to being local and more convenient—generally offer fresher foods in smaller, unpackaged portions. Instead of being loose in bins for the customer to select from, fruits and vegetables will often be pre-sorted into serving baskets. Favorite fruits in Japan are *nashi* (apple pears), *mikan* (mandarin oranges), and *kaki* (persimmons).

第八課 UNIT 8

お風呂　その一

　エィミーは日本の生活にだんだん慣れてきた。もうあまりはずかしがらなくなっていたので、山下一家の人々はよく「エィミーさんはずいぶんはっきりと物を言うようになったね。」と言った。日本の風呂についてエィミーが言ったことなども、そのいい例（れい）かもしれない。

　「ただいま。」玄関でお父さんの声がした。「お帰りなさい。」お母さんはエプロンで手をふきながら玄関に出た。「おつかれさま。」着（き）がえを手伝（てつだ）いながらお母さんがたずねた。「お風呂になさいますか、ご飯になさいますか。」「そうだ

その一　part one
だんだん　gradually
慣れる　to get used to
はっきりと物を言う　to speak frankly
　and openly
〜ようになる　come to do〜, come to
　be that〜
例　an example
〜かもしれない　perhaps, maybe, might〜

ただいま　I'm home
お帰りなさい　welcome home
エプロン　apron
ふく　to wipe
おつかれさま　you must be tired
　(a polite greeting)
着がえ　changing clothes
手伝う　to help, to assist
たずねる　to ask

な。今日は暑かったから先に風呂にしようか。」
お父さんはそう言って風呂場の方へ行った。

「ああ、さっぱりした。」風呂から上がってゆ
かたに着がえたお父さんがテーブルに着いた。
「みんな、ご飯ですよ。」とお母さんが呼んだの
で子供達が二階からおりてきた。

「初めてお風呂に入った時は本当におどろきま
した。」とエィミーが話し始めた。「だってお風
呂場は全部タイルばりだし、お風呂はとても深い
のに、足をのばすにはせま過ぎるんですもの。私
がどう入るのかしらと考えていると明子ちゃんが
『さあ、一緒に入りましょう』と言って服を脱ぎ
だしたでしょう。とてもはずかしかったけれど、

暑い　hot
先に　first
風呂場　bathroom (this term refers only
　　to the place for bathing; toilets are in a
　　separate room)
方へ　toward
さっぱりした　refreshed
（から）上がる　to get up out of
ゆかた　an informal, lightweight cotton
　　kimono for summer wear; a bathrobe
着がえる　to change (into one's clothes)

タイルばり　tiled（ばり = covered, lined）
深い　deep
のに　even though
足　feet, legs
のばす　to stretch out, to extend
～過ぎる　too～, せますぎる= too
　　narrow, cramped
さあ　well, come now
一緒に　together
脱ぎ出す　to start to take off

失礼なことをしてはいけないと思って、私も一緒に服を脱ぎました。

そして湯船に入ろうとしたら、明子ちゃんが『だめだめ、先に外で体を洗って』と言って、湯船の外でお湯で体を洗い始めたんです。せっけんを全然使わずに。それで、私もまねをして体を洗ってからお風呂に入って、思わず『キャッ』と叫びました。お湯がものすごく熱くて体がまっかになりました。それなのに明子ちゃんはとても気持ちよさそうにしているし『熱すぎませんか』と言っても『そうかしら』と言うだけなので私もがまんしました。

明子ちゃんがお風呂から出た時は、ああ、これ

失礼（な）　impolite, rude
湯船　a bathtub
体　body
洗う　to wash
湯　hot water
せっけん　soap
全然　totally ("not at all" with negative verb)
使わずに＝使わないで　without using〜
まねをする　to imitate

思わず　unintentionally, in spite of oneself
キャッと叫ぶ　to yell, to cry out
ものすごく　terribly
熱い　hot
まっか　bright red
それなのに＝それだのに　nevertheless, in spite of this
がまんする　to endure, to exercise one's patience

で終わりだとホッとしました。ところが『さあ、体を洗って』と言って明子ちゃんは細長いタオルのようなものにせっけんをつけて体をゴシゴシ洗い始めたんです。がっかりしたけれど仕方がないから私もその通りにしました。

　せっけんをお湯で流して、さあ今度こそ終わりだと思ったのに、明子ちゃんはまたお風呂に入ったでしょう。日本のお風呂は本当にたいへんだと思いました。」

　「今でもエィミーさんはお風呂はたいへんだと思っているの。」とお母さんが笑いながら聞きました。

　「いいえ、今は好きです。アメリカに帰ったら日本のお風呂がなつかしくなると思います。」とエィミーは答えた。

終わり　an end
ホッとする　to feel relieved
ところが　however
細長い　narrow and long
タオル　towel
ゴシゴシ洗う　to give a good scrub

がっかりする　to feel discouraged, lose heart
仕方がない　it can't be helped
その通り　just the same, just like that
今度こそ　surely this time
なつかしい　to miss (something) fondly

——— 第八課　練習問題 ———

I.　A. 質問に答えなさい

1. エィミーはどのように物をいうようになりましたか。
2. エィミーは初めて日本の風呂に入った時、どう思いましたか。
3. 日本の風呂では足がのばせますか。
4. エィミーと明子は体をせっけんでゴシゴシ洗ってからどうしましたか。
5. 日本人は風呂の中でせっけんを使いますか。
6. エィミーは日本の風呂が好きですか。

B. True or False

1. エィミーははずかしがらないようになりました。
2. お父さんはご飯の前に風呂に入りました。
3. 風呂の中で体を洗います。
4. 風呂の湯はあまり熱くありませんでした。
5. エィミーは初めて風呂に入った時日本の風呂はたいへんだと思いました。

II. 次の質問に答えなさい

1. 日本の風呂の入り方はアメリカの風呂の入り方とどう違いますか。
2. いつか日本の風呂に入りたいですか。

Unit 8 Culture Notes

furo

For the Japanese, bathing is more than a way to get clean. A hot bath is a welcome reward at the end of a long day. It relaxes, refreshes, and renews. The healing, soothing quality of water has long been recognized and appreciated in Japan with a reverence often misunderstood by foreigners. However, most visitors who spend time in Japan come to prefer the Japanese bath to its Western counterpart.

Most Japanese bathe at home, although some still frequent the public baths. The popularity of hot spring resorts throughout the country attests to the pleasure and comfort Japanese find in bathing.

The experience of the *furo* is all the more pleasurable when it is shared. At home the father usually bathes first, either before or after dinner. Some fathers delight in sharing their bath with their young children; bath time may be the only chance for togetherness and play. The mother often bathes last, but may also share the bath with her children, particularly infants.

All washing, scrubbing, and rinsing is done outside the tub, where the bather sits on a short stool or mat-covered board. To wet down or rinse clean, the bather fills a small tub with fresh water from the faucet or hose next to the tub and pours the water all over himself or herself. The tiled or wood floor has a drain.

Because the space for bathing is waterproof and usually enclosed with a sliding glass door, water can be splashed about with abandon. (Sinks and toilets are kept separate from the bathing area.)

After rinsing, the bather carefully steps into the hot water in the tub. Japanese people generally prefer very hot water temperatures. The ideal bath is filled to the rim; as the bather sinks down into the tub, waves of hot water swell and overflow out onto the floor.

The bathtub itself is generally shorter and deeper than an average American tub, so a bather's entire body can be immersed in water. Tubs were once carefully constructed of wood; the fragrant *hinoki* (cypress) was the most favored material. Most tubs are now made of polypropylene reinforced with fiberglass, and some are made of tile. The bath water is heated by gas.

Everyone in the family uses the same water to soak. Since all washing and rinsing is done outside the tub, the bath water stays clean. A lid is kept over the tub to keep the water warm for the next bather. At the end of the evening, the water is let out of the tub or allowed to cool down until it is reheated for bathing again the next day.

Further Reading

Peter Grilli. *Pleasures of the Japanese Bath*. New York: Weatherhill, 1992.

お風呂　その二

エ：「お父さんの子供の頃のお風呂はどんなの
だったんですか。」

父：「そうだねえ、子供の頃、ぼくの家の風呂
は木でできていて底は鉄でね。入る時は木のゆか
の上に乗って入ったんだよ。やけどをしないよう
にね。その風呂は風呂おけの外で火をたいてお湯
をあたためるものだったよ。」

エ：「木で火をたくんですか。すごく熱くあり
ませんでしたか。」

父：「いや、そんなんじゃなくてね。お湯の温
度は気持ちのいいものだった。熱すぎることもぬ
るいこともなくてね。そんな風呂をまだ使ってい

その二　part two
〜頃　about the time when〜
ぼく　I (informal male speech)
底　the bottom
鉄　iron, steel
木のゆか　a wooden platform upon which
　the bather sits (ゆか＝floor)

やけど　a burn
風呂おけ　a bathtub
火をたく　to kindle a fire
いや　no
温度　temperature
ぬるい　lukewarm

る人もいるだろうけれど、ずいぶん少なくなった
だろうね。」

エ：「私は今家で使っているようなのが好きで
す。アメリカのお風呂と同じ材料でできているよ
うで．．．でもアメリカのはもっと長くて、日本
のほど深くはないから全身お湯につかってあたた
まるわけにはいかないでしょう。だから私は日本
のお風呂の方が好きだわ。」

父：「そうそう。銭湯も忘れちゃいけないよ。
昔は風呂のある家は少なかったからみんなが近所
の銭湯に行ったものだ。入り口に銭湯の名前入り
ののれんがかかっていてね、入り口を入るとたい
てい番台に中年のおばさんが座っていた。
男湯と女湯に別れていて、入り口で料金を払っ

少ない　a few
材料　material(s)
全身　the whole body
つかる　to soak
あたたまる　to warm oneself
〜わけにはいかない　there's no way〜
銭湯　public bath*
行ったものだ　used to go

番台　attendant's booth
中年　middle age
男湯　the men's bath
女湯　the women's bath
別れる　to separate
料金　a charge, a fee
払う　to pay

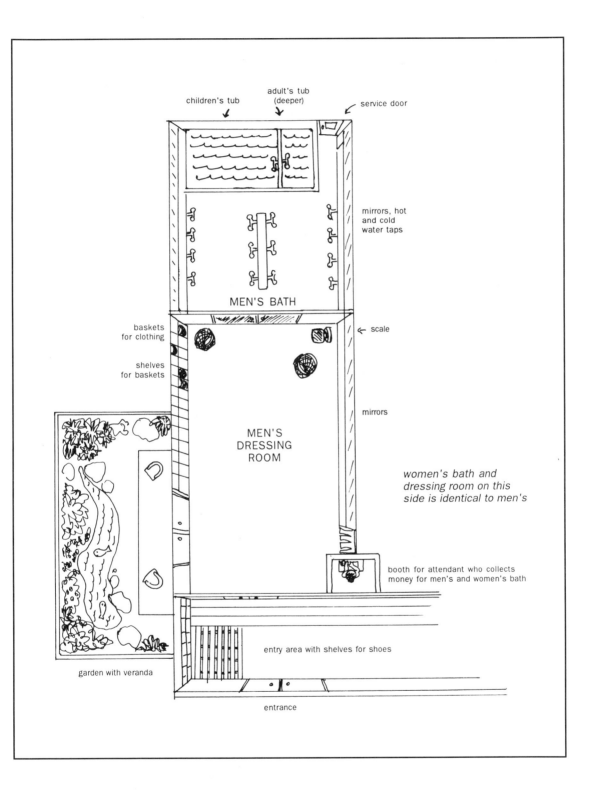

children's tub

adult's tub
(deeper)

service door

mirrors, hot
and cold
water taps

MEN'S BATH

baskets
for clothing

← scale

shelves
for baskets

mirrors

MEN'S
DRESSING
ROOM

*women's bath and
dressing room on this
side is identical to men's*

booth for attendant who collects
money for men's and women's bath

garden with veranda

entry area with shelves for shoes

entrance

てね、靴は入り口のげたばこに入れて、脱衣所で服を脱いで、かごに入れてから風呂場に入ったんだよ。ぼくの行っていた銭湯の壁には富士山の絵が描いてあって、湯船は大きいのが二つあったかな。お湯から上がってからはお年寄がそのへんに座っておしゃべりしながら夕涼みしているのを見てたもんだね。」

エ：「すてきな思い出ですね、お父さん。そんなことをする人はまだいるんですか。」

父：「ああ、でもそれほど多くはないよ。今はほとんどの家に風呂があるから銭湯はあまり必要じゃなくなってきている。でもまだまだ銭湯の好きな人はたくさんいるよ。」

げたばこ　shoe cabinet
脱衣所　a dressing room
かご　basket
壁　wall
富士山　Mt. Fuji
絵　a picture, a painting
描く　to draw, to paint
〜かな　(I) think, guess (wonder)〜

年寄　an elder, an aged person
へん　an area
おしゃべりする　to chatter, to gossip
夕涼みする　to enjoy the cool evening (breeze)
思い出　recollections
ほとんど（の）　most
必要（だ）　necessary

───── 第九課　練習問題 ─────────────

I. A. 質問に答えなさい

1. お父さんが子供の頃、家の風呂はどんなのでしたか。
2. お湯の温度はどうでしたか。
3. まだ昔の風呂を使っている人がいますか。
4. エィミーはどうして今家で使っている風呂の方が好きですか。
5. 昔、風呂のある家が少なかった時みんなはどうしましたか。
6. お父さんの行っていた銭湯はどんなのでしたか。お年寄は風呂から出てから何をしましたか。

B. True or False

1. お父さんが子供の頃、家の風呂は鉄でできていて底は木でした。
2. アメリカの風呂は日本のほど深くはありません。
3. エィミーは日本の風呂よりアメリカの風呂の方が好きです。
4. このごろ銭湯が多くなりました。
5. まだ銭湯の好きな人がたくさんいます。

II. 次の質問に答えなさい

1. あなたは銭湯に行ったことがありますか。それはいつですか。
2. アメリカには銭湯のようなものがありますか。

—————— Unit 9 Culture Notes ——————

sentō

In some modern *sentō*, customers place their street clothes in baskets on shelves or in lockers. They then carry their soap, towels, and other bathing articles into the bathing area.

第十課
UNIT 10

学校の話

　日本の学校の一年は四月に始まって三月に終わる。エィミーは留学生として九月から五月まで一郎の学校に通った。そして他の生徒達と一緒に、歴史、数学、物理、美術などを勉強した。また、茶道部と写真部のクラブ活動にも参加した。十一月末のある日のことだった。

　エ：「ただいま。」

　母：「お帰りなさい。」

　エ：「ああ、つかれた。」

　母：「どうしたの。学校で何かあったの。」

　エ：「いいえ、何も。あの、服を着がえてきます。」

として　as
通う　to attend school
生徒　student ＋ 達＝ students
歴史　history
数学　math
物理　physics

茶道部　tea ceremony club*
写真部　photography club
クラブ　club
活動　activity
参加する　to participate
末　the end of〜

エィミーが台所にもどってくると、お母さんは
エィミーとまゆみにおやつを出してくれた。土曜
日の午後だったので、一郎と明子は友達と出かけ
ていた。まゆみはテーブルの上にノートを広げ
て、一生けんめい絵を描いていた。いすに座って
ためいきをついたエィミーにお母さんが話しかけ
てきた。

　母：「まだ制服に慣れないのね。」

　エ：「どうしてですか。」

　母：「だって、学校から帰るといつもすぐ着が
えるでしょう。」

　エ：「ええ、そうですね。」エィミーはクスク
ス笑いながら言った。

　エ：「制服がいやなわけじゃないんです。でも

もどる　to come back
おやつ　an afternoon snack
午後　afternoon (p.m.)
ノート　a notebook (a shortened form of
　ノートブック)
広げる　to open, to spread out

一生けんめい　as hard as one can, with all
　one's might
ためいきをつく　to sigh
話しかける　to address oneself to someone
クスクス笑う　to giggle, to chuckle
〜わけじゃない　it's not that〜, it's not
　because〜

学校が終わったら楽なかっこうをしたいんで
す。」

　母：「そう、わかったわ。ねえ、エィミーさん
はよく学校の後でお友達と出かけるけど今週はま
だ一度も出かけていないわね。」

　エ：「ええ。何だかちょっとつかれているんで
す。一週間に六日も学校へ行くのに慣れていない
から。それにアメリカにいた時よりも宿題がたく
さんあるんです。それでも私は一郎さんや明子
ちゃんほどは勉強していません。一郎さんは毎晩
四時間くらい、明子ちゃんは三時間くらい勉強し
ているでしょう。そして週に三回じゅくに行って
いるでしょう。」

　母：「この頃の子供はたいへんね。いい大学に
入るために、ようちえんから高校までいい所に行

楽なかっこう　comfortable dress (clothing)
なんだか　somehow
宿題　homework
それでも　however, but
晩　evening

じゅく　private school*
この頃　nowadays
ために　in order for～
ようちえん　kindergarten
高校　senior high school

かなくちゃならないし、いい仕事を見つけるためには、いい大学に行かなくちゃならないんですものね。エィミーさんは『教育ママ』っていう言葉を聞いたことあるかしら。」

エ：「ええ、子供に一日中勉強させるお母さんのことですよね。」

母：「ええ。でも、あれは本当にいいことなのかしらと思ってしまうわ。子供は勉強以外のこともしなくちゃね。一郎は野球をしたりビデオゲームをしたり友達と映画に行ったりするし、明子も映画や買い物に行ったり空手をやったりしているでしょう。それに、家の子は三人ともテレビが好きだし。勉強ばっかりしているよりはいいと思うわ。」

仕事　work	野球　baseball
見つける　to find	映画　a movie
教育ママ　"education mother"	〜たり、たりする　to do such things as〜
言葉　word(s)	空手　karate (a martial art)
一日中　all day long	（三人）とも　all (three people)
以外　outside of, other than	ばっかり　only, just（spoken form of ばかり）

お母さんはさらにぶつぶつと言い続けていた。エィミーはボーッとしていた。お母さんはやはりエィミーが何か困っているのだろうと思った。そしてお茶をつぎ始めたがエィミーは一人になりたかった。「そろそろ部屋にもどって勉強しなくちゃ。」そう言い残してエィミーはゆっくりと階段をのぼっていった。

エィミーは考え事をしながら机に向かっていた。そこに焼きいも屋の声が聞こえてきた。寒くなってから焼きいもはエィミーの大好物になっていた。ホカホカの焼きいもを手にすると、心まであたたまってくるのだった。エィミーの部屋には石油ストーブがあったが、それでもまだ少し寒

さらに　again
ぶつぶつと言う　to grumble, to complain
続ける　to continue
ボーッとする　to be "spaced out," in a daze
やはり　after all, as suspected
困る　to be troubled
つぐ　to pour
一人になる　to be by oneself
そろそろ　soon
言い残す　to leave something unsaid

のぼる　to go up
考え事をする　to think about something
そこに　thereupon
焼きいも　a baked sweet potato*
　＋屋 ＝ a sweet potato vendor
好物　a favorite dish (food)
ホカホカ（の）　warm
手にする　to hold in one's hand(s)
石油ストーブ　a kerosene heater*

かった。「どうしようかな。買いに行こうか
な。」と迷ったが今日はがまんすることにして、
エィミーは机の上の本を開いた。

迷う　to be in doubt

───── 第十課　練習問題 ─────

I. A. 質問に答えなさい
  1. エィミーは学校で何を勉強していましたか。
  2. エィミーは制服をどう思っていますか。それはどうしてですか。
  3. どうしてエィミーはお母さんにつかれているんだと言いましたか。
  4. お母さんはこの頃の子供はどうだと思っていますか。
  5. 「教育ママ」というのは何ですか。
  6. エィミーは焼きいもを買いに行きましたか。

  B. True or False
  1. 日本の学校は三月に始まって四月に終わります。
  2. エィミーはよく学校の後で友達と出かけます。
  3. お母さんによるといい仕事を見つけるためには、いい大学に行かなくてはなりません。
  4. お母さんは子供達が勉強以外のことはしなくてもいいと思っています。
  5. 寒くなってから焼きいもはエィミーの大好物になりました。

II. 次の質問に答えなさい
  1. 日本の学校をどう思いますか。
  2. あなたは学校の勉強以外に何をしますか。

—— Unit 10 Culture Notes ——

sadō

Also called the "Way of Tea," the tea ceremony has had a long history in Japan. With its highly stylized, refined movements and ritualized behavior, it outwardly appears to be a complicated way of making tea, a "polite" accomplishment for Japanese women. However, *sadō* is generally regarded as a spiritual discipline, greatly influenced by Zen Buddhism. Through practice, the ideal is to develop peace within oneself and the world, respect for life, and the ability to cherish the uniqueness of every moment.

Further Reading

Kakuzo Okakura. *The Book of Tea.* Rutland, VT, and Tokyo: Charles E. Tuttle, 1956.

Soshitsu Sen. *Tea Life, Tea Mind.* New York: Weatherhill, 1979.

juku

There are many types of study schools, or *juku*, operating in Japan today. Some are national chains and others are privately owned. Some specialize in university entrance examination subjects such as English, math, and Japanese. Still others are known for the arts and sports.

yaki-imo

In the winter, street vendors often sell these light yellow and mildly sweet potatoes fresh from steamers in the rear of their trucks. The driver calls out "*Yaki-imo*" through a loudspeaker as he drives slowly down the street. Many Japanese find it a delight to hold and eat a hot sweet potato on a cold day.

sekiyu-sutōbu

Most homes in Japan do not have central heating, so kerosene or electric space heaters are used to heat only those rooms which are in use at the moment. Japan's major fuel resource is petroleum. Since 99% of this must be imported, the cost of fuel is very high. Japanese are very conscientious about conserving fuel.

第十一課 UNIT 11　エィミーのなやみ

　その日の夜遅く、十二時ごろに、エィミーはいやな夢を見て目を覚ました。台所ではまだ食器のカタカタする音がしていた。しばらくしてエィミーが下におりていくと、お母さんが眠そうに目をこすりながら本を読んでいた。

　母：「エィミーさん。こんなに遅くまで何をしているの。」

　エ：「眠れないんです。お母さんこそつかれているみたいなのに...どうして寝ないんですか。」

　母：「お父さんを待っているのよ。会社の人達とお出かけだから。」

なやみ　trouble, worry, fear	しばらくして　after a little while
夜　night	眠そうに　sleepily
遅く　late	目をこする　to rub one's eyes
夢　a dream	寝る　to sleep
夢を見る　to dream	会社　a company
目を覚ます　to be awake	お出かけ　（出かける）to go out
カタカタする　to clatter	

エ：「でも、お母さんとてもつかれているみたいですよ。」

母：「ええ、でもお父さんがおなかをすかして帰っていらっしゃるかもしれないし。」

エ：「お父さんは自分で何か作れないんですか。」

母：「とんでもない。それに料理は私の仕事だから。」

エ：「そうですか。日本の習慣なんでしょうね。私にはまだよくわからないけれど。」

母：「そうかもしれないわね。ねえ、エィミーさん、お茶でも飲まない。」

エ：「じゃあ、いただきます。」

エィミーはパジャマのままで、お母さんの横に座った。前から聞きたいと思っていたことが頭に浮かんだ。

おなかをすかす　to feel (get) hungry
とんでもない　no way! out of the question!
料理　cooking, cuisine

パジャマ　pajamas
パジャマのままで　while still in pajamas
頭に浮かぶ　to occur to one's mind

エ：「お母さん、どうして留学生を家に置くこ
とにしたんですか。」

母：「そうね。ええと、私達はみんなアメリカ
という国にとても興味を持っていたの。それで
ね、アメリカの人がどんなふうに考えるかが知り
たくなったのね。でもそれがどうかしたの。」

エ：「いいえ、ただ。私にも何人か日本人の友
達がいるでしょう。時々一緒に音楽を聞いたり買
い物に行ったりする友達が。」

母：「それで。」

エ：「なんだかその人達は私がアメリカ人だか
ら友達になったような気がするんです。もしも私
が中国人だったら友達になったかしらなんて思っ
てしまうんです。あの人達は、ただ英会話の練習
がしたくて、私の友達になったんでしょうか。本

置く　to put, to place (to have, in this case)　　気がする　to think, to have a feeling that
（そんな）ふう　(that) way　　英会話　English conversation
音楽　music

当に友達になりたいのか、アメリカの友達がいるのはカッコイイからなのかわからなくなってしまったんです。」

　母：「まあ、エィミーさん、そんなこと．．．」

　お母さんはしばらくだまって考えていたが、やがてこう言った。

　母：「エィミーさん、あなたがそんなふうに思っていたなんて知らなかったわ。私達は、エィミーさんが家に来てくれてとても喜んでいるのよ。エィミーさんのお友達だって、本当にあなたのことが好きなんだと思うんだけど。今はまだ来たばかりだから色々な思いをすると思うけれど、しばらくすれば、私が今言ったことがわかると思うわ。」

　エィミーとお母さんはそれからもう少し話し

カッコイイ　(it) "looks good," is fashionable
だまる　to be silent
やがて　before long

まだ来たばかり　(you've) but just arrived
色々な思いをする　to have various experiences
しばらくすれば　in a short time

た。エィミーはお母さんが自分の気持ちをわかっ
てくれたのがうれしかった。心が軽くなって、二
階の部屋にもどった。エィミーはとても眠かった
ので横になった。台所ではお母さんが目をこすり
ながらまた本を読み始めた。

心が軽くなる　to feel relieved

———— 第十一課　練習問題 ————

I. A. 質問に答えなさい
1. エィミーが下におりて行った時お母さんは何をしていましたか。
2. お母さんはどうして遅くまで起きていましたか。
3. お母さんはどうしてお父さんを待っていましたか。
4. どうして山下さん一家は留学生を家に置くことにしましたか。
5. エィミーのなやみは何ですか。

B. True or False
1. エィミーはいやな夢を見ました。
2. 料理はお父さんの仕事です。
3. お母さんは本を読みたかったので起きていました。
4. 山下さん一家はアメリカに興味を持っていました。
5. エィミーは日本の友達は彼女がアメリカ人だから友達になったと思っていました。
6. 山下さん一家はエィミーが家にいるのをとてもいやがっています。
7. エィミーはお母さんと少し話して心が軽くなりました。

II. 次の質問に答えなさい
あなたの家では料理はだれの仕事ですか。お母さんのですか、
お父さんのですか。

——— Unit 11 Culture Notes ———

daidokoro

The kitchen in a Japanese home is usually packed with electrical gadgets. Probably the most important of these is the rice cooker, which is designed to cook rice perfectly every time (and to hold enough so that everyone can get second or third helpings if they want).

お正月

お母さんと相談してから、数週間が過ぎた。エィミーは家の人達とうまくいっていたし、学校も楽しんでいた。少しホームシックにかかっていたが、エィミーは元気だった。

（１２月３０日）

みんなが朝食を食べていた。正月の二日前の日のことである。

エ：「とうとうお正月ですね。どんな準備をするんですか。」

父：「そうだね、今日はしょうじをはりかえなくちゃいけないね。」

正月　the New Year
二日　two days
相談する　to discuss, to talk over
　(something with someone)
〜（と）うまくいく　to do well with〜

ホームシックにかかる　to get homesick
とうとう　at last
準備（を）する　to make preparations
しょうじ　see Unit 3 Culture Notes
はりかえる　to repaper (a *shōji*)

107

母：「そうですね。それに、おそうじと、おせちの準備もしなくちゃなりませんよ。お正月の三が日はお料理やおそうじができませんからね。」

エ：「それは、お正月には休むことになっているからですか。」

母：「ええ。それにお正月には福の神が家の中に入ってくるから、それをはきだしてしまわないようにするためもあるのよ。」

エィミーとまゆみはお父さんがしょうじをはりかえるのを手伝った。気をつけてしょうじ紙をはがした後に、お母さんの作ってくれたのりで新しい紙を貼った。その後で、エィミーは自分の部屋のたたみをふいて、さらにお母さんが居間のそうじをするのを手伝った。大そうじが終わるとお母

そうじ　cleaning
おせち＝せち料理　dishes for the New Year*
三が日　the first three days of the New Year
〜ことになる　it is decided that〜,
　　supposed to be that〜
福　(good) fortune, luck, happiness, blessing
神　god, God, divinity, divine being, spirit*
はき出す　to sweep out
〜ようにする　to make sure that〜

気をつける　to be careful
紙　paper
はがす　to peel off
のり　paste, glue
貼る　to stick, to paste, to affix
たたみ　see Unit 3 Culture Notes
ふく　to mop (wipe) up
大そうじ　a thorough house-cleaning

さん、エィミー、まゆみ、明子の四人はおせち料理
の準備をしてそれをていねいに重箱につめた。おせ
ち料理の他には、寿司やたいなどが準備された。

　母：「エィミーさん、たいっていう魚知ってい
る。」

　エ：「いいえ、何ですか。」

　母：「たいっていうのはね、おめでたい時に食
べるお魚なの。たいっていう名前は、おめでたい
のたいと同じ音でしょう。」

　その後お母さんと明子はエィミーに日本の歌を
教え、みんなは準備をしながらその歌を歌った。

　母：「エィミーさん、玄関にお鏡を置いてきて
くれない。」

　エ：「はい。お鏡って、おもしろい形をしてい
ますね。」

重箱　a tiered box traditionally made
　of lacquered wood or porcelain
つめる　to cram, to fill
寿司　vinegared rice and fish
たい　a sea bream (a type of fish)

（お）めでたい　happy, joyous, propitious
歌　a song
歌う　to sing
お鏡＝鏡もち　a round, mirror-shaped rice
　cake（an offering)*

母：「あら、見るのは初めて。」

エ：「ええ、初めてです。」

エィミーは鏡もちを玄関に置きに行った。居間でみんなが一休みしていた。お母さんが「お茶が入りましたよ。」と言った。

エ：「おおみそかの晩は何をするんですか。」

父：「近くのお寺に除夜の鐘を聞きに行かないか。」

エ：「除夜の鐘って何ですか。」

父：「お寺でおおみそかに鳴らす鐘のことだよ。百八回鳴らすんだ。これは一年間の災いを全部取り除くといわれているんだ。」

エ：「それはおもしろそうですね。みなさんも行くんですか。」

あら　an exclamation of surprise (female speech)
一休みする　to take a short rest
おおみそか　the last day of the year (New Year's Eve)
寺　a Buddhist temple

除夜の鐘　a temple bell which rings out the old year on New Year's Eve
鳴らす　to ring (a bell)
百八回　one hundred and eight times
災い　misfortune
取り除く　to remove

　明：「私達は紅白歌合戦を見ているわ。でもまゆみはお父さんやエィミーと一緒に行くんじゃないかしら。」

　まゆみ：「私、行く。」

　エ：「じゃ、一緒に行きましょうね。とても楽しそうだわ。」

紅白歌合戦　a singing competition between
　two teams called the "reds" and the "whites,"
　broadcast every New Year's Eve on NHK, a
　major public television network

——— 第十二課　練習問題 ———

I. A. 質問に答えなさい
1. 正月の前にはどんな準備をしなければなりませんか。
2. どうして正月の三が日は料理やそうじができませんか。
3. おせち料理の他にはどんな食べ物を準備しますか。
4. エィミーは玄関に何を置きに行きましたか。
5. おおみそかの晩みんなは何をしますか。
6. 除夜の鐘というのは何ですか。

B. True or False
1. エィミーは家の人達とうまくいっていません。
2. 正月には福の神が家の中に入ってきます。
3. 正月の前にはしょうじをはりかえます。
4. エィミーとお父さんと明子はおおみそかの夜、寺に行きます。
5. まゆみとお母さんと一郎はその夜紅白歌合戦を見ます。

II. 次の質問に答えなさい
あなたの家では正月のためにとくべつな食べ物を食べますか。
それは何ですか。

──── Unit 12 Culture Notes ────

osechi-ryōri

Osechi consists of a variety of cold dishes for the New Year, beautifully arranged in a three- or four-tiered lacquered or porcelain box called a *jūbako. Osechi* is prepared in advance and eaten cold so that New Year's Day can be a day for celebration and rest. The following are three examples of regional *osechi* dishes:

kurikinton

A thick mixture of chestnuts and sugar to which Japanese sweet potatoes are sometimes added.

konbu-maki

A filling of fish or meat is rolled up in *konbu* (a type of sea vegetable) and tied with a long thin strip of dried gourd called *kanpyō.* The *konbu* rolls are then cooked in a mixture of soy sauce, sugar, and fish stock.

renkon

These lotus roots are either cooked in fish stock, soy sauce, and sugar or are pickled in vinegar with sugar and red food coloring.

kami

Kami are the focus of ritual worship and celebration in Shinto. See Stuart D. B. Picken, *Shinto: Japan's Spiritual Roots* (Tokyo and New York: Kodansha International, 1980).

kagami-mochi

Balls of steamed, pounded rice called *mochi* are placed on white paper on top of a wooden stand (*sanbō*), which is often decorated with an orange and a fern or piece of *konbu.* This offering usually sits on a shelf or shoe cabinet just inside the *genkan.*

第十三課 UNIT 13　　　　　除夜の鐘

　お父さんはエィミーとまゆみを近所のお寺に連れていった。りんとした空気の中で大きいかがり火がもえていた。むらさきと金色のきれいな衣を着たおぼうさん達がお勤めをしていた。一人のおぼうさんが大きいなべから甘酒を配っていた。みんながこの熱くて甘い飲み物を飲んで、体をあたためていた。お父さんがエィミーに「甘酒は体にいいんだよ。」と言った。

　除夜の鐘が始まる前に、さんけいしゃは自由に鐘をつくことができた。鐘の前にはたくさんの人

りんとした　clear and crisp
空気　air
かがり火　bonfire
もえる　to burn
むらさき　purple
金色　gold color
衣　a priest's robe
（お）ぼうさん（＝ぼうず）　a priest, monk
勤め　duty, task　（勤めをする＝ to attend to one's duties). In the case of high-ranking monks, "duty" implies "prayer,"
while lower-ranking monks would be welcoming visitors and keeping the wood burning.
なべ　a pot　（大きいなべ＝ cauldron）
甘酒　a sweet drink made from fermented rice
配る　to distribute
甘い　sweet
さんけいしゃ　visitors to a shrine or temple
自由に　freely
つく　to strike　(a bell)

が列を作っていた。エィミーはボーイスカウトの子供達の後ろに並んだ。とうとうエィミーの番が来た。ワクワクしながら、つるされた長い丸太のはじに付けられたロープを手に持って、鐘をついた。鐘の音は大きく澄んでいてとてもきれいだった。

お父さんがまゆみが鐘をつくのを手伝った後で、三人はかがり火の前に立った。いよいよおぼうさんが除夜の鐘を打ち始めた。人々はみんなだまって一つ一つの鐘の音に聞き入っていた。百八つの鐘が鳴り終わるとまわりの人々は歓声をあげた。エィミーも思わずまゆみを抱き上げていた。

三人は家に帰った。家中の者がこたつのまわりに集まって、年こしそばを食べた。そのころには

列を作る　to line up
ボーイスカウトの子供達　boy scouts
並ぶ　to stand in line
番が来た　(her) turn came
ワクワクする　to get excited
つるす　to suspend
丸太　a log
はじに付ける　to attach to an end
ロープ　a rope
澄む　to become clear
いよいよ　at long last

打つ　to strike, to hit
一つ一つ　one by one
聞き入る　to listen attentively
鳴る　to ring
まわり　surrounding
歓声をあげる　to shout for joy, to let out a cheer
抱き上げる　to take up in one's arms
家中の者　all the family members
こたつ　*
年こしそば　New Year's Eve buckwheat noodles*

エィミーもはしの使い方がうまくなっていた。一郎が言った。

一郎：「エィミーさん、今日はそばをこぼしていないじゃないか。ずいぶんうまくなったね。」

エィミーは初めてそばを食べた日を思い出してニコニコした。

こぼす　to drop
ずいぶん　really

ニコニコする　to smile radiantly, to beam

—— 第十三課　練習問題 ——

I. A. 質問に答えなさい
1. おぼうさんは何をしていましたか。
2. 甘酒とは何ですか。
3. エィミーはどうやって鐘をつきましたか。
4. 百八つの鐘が鳴り終わるとまわりの人々は何をしましたか。
5. 三人は家に帰った後で何をしましたか。

B. True or False
1. 甘酒は体にいいです。
2. さんけいしゃは自由に除夜の鐘をつくことができました。
3. 鐘の音はきれいでした。
4. みんなはこたつのまわりでたいを食べました。
5. エィミーははしの使い方が上手になりました。

II. 次の質問に答えなさい
あなたは正月に何をしますか。

—————— Unit 13 Culture Notes ——————

kotatsu

A *kotatsu* is a small floor-level table or desk with a radiant heating unit attached to its underside. A blanket between the top surface and the frame is used to help contain the heat around the legs and stomach of the person sitting at the *kotatsu*.

toshikoshi-soba

This very long buckwheat noodle symbolizes longevity. It is served in a broth with vegetables, and sometimes with fish cakes called *kamaboko*.

第十四課 UNIT 14 　　　　　　　　 がんじつ 元日

元日の食卓は、新年用に特別きれいにかざられていた。はし置きまで、いつもと違うものが使われていた。新年のあいさつをかわした後で、みんなはきれいなぬりのおわんに入ったおぞうにや色々な正月料理を食べた。エィミーはおぞうにに入っている自分の切った花形のにんじんを見て、ほこらしく思った。

朝食の後でみんながくつろいでいる時に、お母さんが言った。

母：「エィミーさん、着物を着てみない。」

元日　New Year's Day
食卓　dining table
新年　the New Year
かざる　to decorate
はし置き　chopstick holder
あいさつをかわす　to exchange greetings
（お）ぞうに　a soup for New Year's morning consisting of small pieces of mochi and vegetables in a lightly seasoned broth

切る　to cut
花形　flower-shaped
にんじん　carrot
ほこらしく思う　to feel proud
くつろぐ　to relax and make oneself comfortable

エ：「わあ、うれしい。でも、私のサイズの着物があるんですか。」

母：「あら、着物にはほとんどサイズがないのよ。着物はどんな人にでも着られるようにできているの。」　お母さん、明子、まゆみ、エィミーは、お互いに着物を着るのを助け合った。

エ：「着物を着るのにこんなにひもがいるなんて知りませんでした。着物って重くてきゅうくつなんですね。」

母：「あら、エィミーさん、着るのがいやになったの。」

エ：「とんでもない。こんなにきれいなんですもの、とてもうれしいです。ただ、着るのがあんまりたいへんなので、おどろいているんです。」

母：「そうね、たしかにたいへんね。この頃は

サイズ　size
助け合う　to help one another
ひも　a string, a cord
いる　to need, to be necessary
重い　heavy

きゅうくつ（な）　tight, cramped, uncomfortable
とんでもない　not at all
あんまり　emphatic form of あまり
おどろく　to be surprised
たしかに　certainly

日本人でも自分で着物を着られない人が多くて、着方を教える学校まであるんですものね。」

エ：「こうして自分で着てみると、その理由<ruby>理由<rt>りゆう</rt></ruby>がよくわかります。」

母：「あらあらエィミーさん、だめよ、そんなふうに歩いちゃ。」

エ：「えっ、歩き方まで違うんですか。着物って本当にたいへんなんですね。」

理由　a reason　　　　　　　　だめよ．．．歩いちゃ＝．．．歩いてはだめ

第十四課　練習問題

I A. 質問に答えなさい
1．元日の食卓はいつものとどう違いますか。
2．元日の朝食には何を食べましたか。
3．着物にはサイズがありますか。
4．エィミーは着物を着た時どうしておどろきましたか。
5．エィミーは着物を着るのが好きでしたか。

B. True or False
1．おぞうにには花形のにんじんが入っていました。
2．着物には色々なサイズがあります。
3．この頃自分で着物を着られない日本人がたくさんいます。
4．着物を着ると歩き方が違います。

II. 次の質問に答えなさい
着物を着たことがありますか。
あったら、それはいつですか。
なかったら、着てみたいですか。
どうしてですか。

—— Unit 14 Culture Notes ——

ozōni A fish-based broth to which vegetables and *mochi* are added. It is served in special lacquered bowls.

kimono This traditional manner of dress is now usually reserved for special occasions such as holidays, weddings, visits to shrines and temples, tea gatherings, and traditional musical or theatrical events. The *kimono* and its accessories are very expensive and require special care and laundering. The *kimono* is also heavy and restricts the body's movement, making it an impractical garment for daily use.

The *kimono* is tailored to one standard pattern but varies greatly in color, texture, and design. *Kimono* are made of cotton, synthetic blends, or silk. Styles of embroidery, stitching, stenciling, waxing, and tie-dying techniques are often associated with and identify a province or locality.

The *kimono* is worn with a sashlike accessory called an *obi*. The *obi* is approximately one foot wide and eight feet long and can be wrapped around the waist and tied in several different ways. An amazing variety of clips, cords, and velcro help keep the *kimono* and *obi* together.

Other accessories include footwear such as *tabi* and *zōri*. *Tabi* are ankle-high socks made of a cloth that is thicker and smoother than the cloth of regular cotton socks. Women wear white *tabi* while men may wear black or navy. *Tabi* are distinctive for their "indent" between the big toe and the second toe. This indent conveniently accommodates the sandal-like thong of the *zōri*, the type of footwear most often worn with the *kimono*.

The color and design of the *kimono* vary according to the age and sex of the wearer. For example, young girls wear bright shades of red, green, blue, yellow, and orange. Young women continue to wear bright colors, but as they get older they wear more pastel and subdued colors and designs. Grandmothers wear shades of gray and silver. Men and boys wear darker colors with less obvious designs and thinner *obi*.

A *kimono* can also reflect the season in which it is worn. Bright red maple leaves are patterns for fall, while plum blossom designs are worn in early spring.

第十五課
UNIT 15

はつもうで
初詣

「おおい、そろそろ初詣（はつもうで）に行かないか。」とお父さんが言ったので、みんなは車に乗って、近くの神社（じんじゃ）へ行った。神社（じんじゃ）にはたくさんの人が車で来ていたので、山下さん一家は駐車（ちゅうしゃ）してからかなり歩かなければならなかった。人の波（なみ）に押（お）されるようにして鳥居（とりい）をくぐった後で、一行（いっこう）は手水（てみず）やで手を清（きよ）めた。明子がひしゃくを取って、手の清（きよ）め方をエィミーに教えてくれた。

　神社（じんじゃ）のけいだいは、食べ物、おもちゃ、土産物（みやげもの）などを売る屋台（やたい）がたくさん出ていて活気（かっき）に満（み）ちて

初詣　the first shrine visit of the year
おおい　hey!
神社　a Shinto shrine
駐車する　to park (a car)
かなり　considerably
波　wave(s)
押す　to push, to press
～ようにする　to do (something) in such
　a way that～
鳥居　a Shinto shrine gateway*

一行　a party (the "Yamashita party" or group)
手水や　a water basin*
手を清める　to cleanse one's hands
ひしゃく　a dipper (made from materials such
　as bamboo, finely shaved wood or metal)
けいだい　the precincts, the grounds
売る　to sell
屋台（店）　an open air stall, a booth for
　selling things
活気に満ちる　to be full of spirit and life

いた。しゃてき、だるまおとしといったゲームまであった。まゆみにせがまれてエィミーはわなげにちょうせんすることにした。

しばらく遊んだ後で、一行は本でんへ行き、順番を待ってからおさいせんをささげ、新年の安全とけんこうを祈った。

エ：「初めて神社へ来た時は、建物の外でお祈りをするのでおどろきました。アメリカの教会では建物の中でお祈りをしますから。」

母：「そうなの。本当に違うのね。神様を呼ぶのに鈴を鳴らすのはどう。」

エ：「おもしろいと思います。」

おまいりが済んでから一行はけいだいの茶屋に

_____

しゃてき　target practice
だるまおとし　*
せがむ　to badger(someone to do
　something)
わなげ　ringtoss
ちょうせんする　to challenge (someone)
本でん　a main (inner) shrine
順番を待つ　to await one's turn
（お）さいせん　a money offering
ささげる　to give (in a devotional sense)

安全　safety, security
けんこう　health
祈る　to pray
建物　a building
教会　church
鈴　bell*
（お）まいり　a visit to a temple (shrine),
　to worship
済む　to end, to finish
茶屋　a tea stand

寄って、お茶を飲みながらおしゃべりをした。

　家に帰ってからみんなはおせち料理を食べたり
年賀状を読んだりした。年始まわりの客が何人か
やってきた。大人達は酒を飲み始めた。明子と一
郎は、エィミーにけんだまやはねつきを教えてく
れた。

寄る　to approach, to gather (at)
年賀状　a New Year's card*
年始まわりの客　New Year's guests
大人　an adult

酒　liquor
けんだま　a cup and ball game*
はねつき　a game similar to badminton*

—— 第十五課　練習問題 ——

I. A. 質問に答えなさい
　　1. 初詣というのは何のことですか。
　　2. みんなは鳥居をくぐった後で何をしましたか。
　　3. 神社のけいだいにはどんな物がありましたか。
　　4. みんなは本でんで何をしましたか。
　　5. 家に帰ってからみんなは何をしましたか。

　B. True or False
　　1. 近くの神社はとても込んでいました。
　　2. 手水やでは手を清めます。
　　3. 日本の神社ではさんけいしゃは建物の中で祈ります。
　　4. 年始まわりの客はだれもやってきませんでした。
　　5. 明子と一郎とエィミーはけんだまやはねつきをして遊びました。

II. 次の質問に答えなさい
　　あなたは日本人のお祈りのし方をどう思いますか。

—— Unit 15 Culture Notes ——

torii

This gatelike structure marks sacred space in and around a Shinto shrine. It also serves as a symbol for the shrine.

temizuya

Water basins, common to Shinto shrines, are used for symbolic cleansing. Visitors use a dipper for water to rinse their hands before approaching the main sanctuary and offering prayers.

daruma-otoshi

This game features the figure of Daruma (Bodhidharma), an Indian monk of the sixth century A.D. who taught Buddhism in China. The figure consists of a face sitting on top of a series of flat blocks that form the rest of the monk's body. The object of the game is to strike at each block successively with a small wooden hammer without toppling Daruma's head. Daruma represents spiritual calm and balance. Some Daruma dolls are rounded at the bottom so that when knocked over, they always bounce back. Many Japanese hope that they, like the Daruma figure, can also "bounce back" from any disturbance or trouble life may bring.

suzu o narasu

The center front of a shrine has a long rope suspended from the eaves of the roof. Bells are attached at the top of this rope. Worshipers tug the rope to ring the bells, clap their hands twice, and then silently bow their heads in prayer.

nengajō

These New Year's cards resemble post cards and are sent to relatives, friends, and acquaintances. Businesses send them to customers. Some families design their own cards and have them specially printed. It is not unusual to send out dozens or even hundreds of *nengajō.* The post office delivers the cards on New Year's Day, a time when family and friends traditionally visit one another to pay their respects and exchange good wishes for the year.

kendama

This wooden toy has a handle on one end, a spike at the other, and a cup on each side of the shaft. A ball with a hole in it is attached by a string to the handle. The object is to toss the ball up and catch it on the spike and cups in different sequences. *Kendama* is not traditionally known as a New Year's game.

hanetsuki

This game, played on New Year's Day, has its origins in the fifteenth century. The game uses a wooden paddle (usually elaborately decorated) and a shuttlecock and can be played alone or with another player. With one player, the aim is to keep the shuttlecock in the air; played by two people, the game resembles badminton.

第十六課
UNIT 16

入学式　その一
（にゅうがくしき）

　冬はあっという間に終わった。三月末の春休みの初日のことだった。エィミーは近所を歩きながら桜（さくら）のかおりを楽しんでいた。「今週は京都（きょうと）に行ってお寺やお庭（にわ）を見よう。」「みんなとお花見（はなみ）に行くのもいいな。」あれこれ考えているうちに心が自然（しぜん）にウキウキしてきた。

　エィミーが家にもどった時、お母さんは庭（にわ）で洗濯物（せんたくもの）を干（ほ）していた。

　エ：「ただいま。」

　母：「お帰りなさい。」

　エ：「みんなはどこ。」

入学式　an entrance ceremony (for school)
あっという間に　all of a sudden
初日　a first day
桜　cherry tree (cherry blossoms)*
かおり　fragrance
京都　an imperial capital of Japan
　　(A.D. 794–1868), famous for its
　　traditional architecture, gardens, and art

庭　garden, yard*
花見　cherry blossom viewing
〜うちに　while〜
自然に　naturally
ウキウキする　to be cheerful and lighthearted
洗濯物　laundry
干す　to dry

母：「一郎と明子は外へ遊びに行っているわ。」

二人が話しているところへ、家の中からまゆみの声が聞こえてきた。

ま：「お母さん、おばあちゃんから小包が来た。」

二人が居間に行くと、まゆみがビリビリと包紙を破っているところだった。

母：「まゆみ、だめよ。そんなにらんぼうにしちゃ。」

お母さんはそう言うと、ていねいにひもをほどき始めた。

ま：「おばあちゃん、何を送ってくれたのかな。」

母：「さあ、何かしらね。」

～ているところだ　to be in the midst of doing something
小包　a package
ビリビリと破る　to rip to shreds
包紙　wrapping paper

～ているところだった　was in the midst of doing something
らんぼうする　to be rough
ほどく　to untie
送る　to send

ま：「あっ、ランドセルだ、ランドセルだ。」

母：「よかったわね、まゆみ。これで学校へ行けるわね。」

エ：「まゆみちゃん、しょってみないの。」

エィミーの言葉にうながされて、まゆみはランドセルをしょった。そして、ニコニコしながら部屋の中をグルグル歩き回った。まゆみは体が小さかったので、まるでランドセルが歩いているように見えた。

母：「もう、小学生になったみたいね。」

エ：「そうですね。入学式は来週でしょう。」

ま：「うん。」

母：「まゆみ、せっかくおばあちゃんがくださったんだから、大切にしなくちゃね。」

ま：「うん。」

ランドセル　a sturdy leather knapsack used for books*
しょう　to carry (something) on one's back
うながす　to prompt, to urge (someone to do～)

グルグル歩き回る　to walk around and around
まるで　as if
小学生　a primary school student
せっかく　with much trouble and effort
大切にする　to value (something)

エ：「私からもまゆみちゃんにお祝いがあるの
よ。たいしたものじゃないけど。」

そう言いながらエィミーはきれいなリボンのか
かった包みを、まゆみにわたした。中からスヌー
ピーのついた赤い筆入れが出てきた。

ま：「わっ、このスヌーピー、まゆみ大好き。
どうもありがとう。」

エ：「どういたしまして。一生けんめい勉強し
てね。」

それからお母さんはまゆみのかばんや文房具な
どに名前を書いたり、体育着に名前をぬいつけた
りでいそがしくなった。

入学式の日が来た。お母さんは他にもする事が
たくさんあったので、大急ぎで朝ご飯のしたくを

（お）祝い（物）　a gift (for celebration)
たいしたもの　a valuable thing, a treasure
リボン　ribbon (リボンのかかる〜＝
　〜to be tied with a ribbon)
わたす　to hand over
スヌーピー　Snoopy
筆入れ　pencil case

かばん　satchel
文房具　stationery, writing materials
体育着　a gym uniform
ぬいつける　to sew on
大急ぎで　in a big hurry
したくをする　to prepare for

した。居間ではお父さんがまゆみに話していた。

父：「まゆみ、お父さんは一緒に入学式に行け
ないけど、もう今日から一年生なんだからちゃん
とするんだぞ、いいな。」

ま：「はい。」

まゆみは少しきんちょうしているようだった。
エィミーがスヌーピーの絵を描いて、それに「お
めでとう」と書いて、まゆみにわたした。それを
見てまゆみは笑った。

お母さんがまゆみに新しいワンピースを着せて
白いタイツをはかせた。エィミーは黄色いぼうし
をまゆみにかぶせた。新しい服がうれしくてまゆ
みは外に出て、家の前でスキップをしていた。

一年生　first grader
ちゃんとする　to do well and properly
〜ぞ　"listen to me," "I'm telling you"
きんちょうする　to be tense
ワンピース　a one-piece dress
着せる　to clothe, to dress

白い　white
タイツ　tights
ぼうし　a hat*
かぶせる　to put on (a hat)
スキップをする　to skip

────── 第十六課　練習問題 ──────

I.　A. 質問に答えなさい
　　1. エィミーは春休みの間にどんなことをしたがっていましたか。
　　2. おばあさんから何が来ましたか。
　　3. まゆみはエィミーに何をもらいましたか。
　　4. お父さんは入学式に行きますか。
　　5. まゆみが少しきんちょうしていた時エィミーは何をしましたか。
　　6. まゆみの入学式のための服は何ですか。

　　B. True or False
　　1. エィミーは近所を歩きながら花見のことを考えていましたか。
　　2. まゆみは包紙をビリビリと破りました。
　　3. まゆみは明子と一郎からお祝いをもらいました。
　　4. まゆみがきんちょうしているようだったからエィミーは「がんばってください」と言いました。
　　5. お母さんは入学式のための新しい服を着ました。

II. 次の質問に答えなさい
　　初めて学校に行った日のこと覚えていますか。子供達はどんな
　　気持ちでしょうか。

——— Unit 16 Culture Notes ———

sakura

The cherry blossom is Japan's national symbol. Because *sakura* bloom for only a short time before they fall to the ground, they represent for the Japanese the uniqueness and preciousness of the moment, the change and flow of life, purity and simplicity.

The Japanese look forward every year to the "viewing" of cherry blossoms. Families, friends, and coworkers celebrate this national pastime by picnicking beneath flowering cherry trees in parks, along riverbanks and at temples. Some companies reserve particular spots in advance in order to hold *sake* parties outdoors for their employees. In the spring, weather forecasts feature reports on where and when *sakura* will be in bloom.

niwa

Most city homes do not have a yard, but there is often a small space behind the house graced with beautiful stones or rocks, a few plants, or *bonsai*. Because of limited space, laundry is often hung in the *niwa*. This type of *niwa* is not to be confused with the special gardens of temples and shrines.

randoseru

A *randoseru* is a high-quality leather knapsack for carrying books and school supplies. It is sturdy enough to last through at least six years of school.

bōshi

Bōshi generally means "hat," but in this unit it refers specifically to the bright caps children wear so they can be easily spotted by motorists. This is especially important since many narrow neighborhood streets do not have sidewalks.

第十七課
UNIT 17

入学式 その二

　お母さんとエィミーはまゆみと一緒に学校まで歩いた。空は青く晴れていて散りかけの桜がそよ風にまっていた。

　学校に着くと二人はまゆみを一年三組の教室に連れていった。教室にはたんにんの田中先生や手伝いの上級生がいた。真新しい服を着た新入生ももう何人か来ていた。教室の後ろの方にはお父さんやお母さん達が心配そうな顔をして立っていた。

　しばらくするとベルが鳴った。新入生が廊下に並んでから、先生は体育館に連れていった。そし

青い　blue
晴れる　to become clear
散りかけの桜　falling cherry blossoms
そよ風　a gentle breeze
まう　to flutter about, to dance
組　class, group
教室　classroom
たんにんの先生　a teacher in charge

上級生　an upper-class student
真新しい　brand new
新入生　a new student
しばらくすると　after a while
ベル　a bell
廊下　a hallway
体育館　gymnasium

てクラスごとに座らせられた。エィミーとお母さんは後ろの父兄席に座った。前の方にまゆみの小さい体が見えた。

　いよいよ入学式が始まった。まず校長先生があいさつをした。先生は学校の年中行事について話した後で先生方を紹介した。次にＰＴＡの会長があいさつをした。その後で何人かのらいひんがあいさつをした。一生けんめい勉強するように新入生をはげましたが大人の話はどれもむずかしくてまゆみにはよくわからなかった。まゆみはたいくつして早く式が終わればいいと思った。

　上級生が校歌を歌って式は終わった。まゆみは先頭に立って教室に帰ってきた。教室で生徒は先生から教科書などをもらい、みんなの前で一人ず

クラス　class
ごとに　each
父兄席　seats for parents and siblings
いよいよ　finally
校長先生　a principal
年中行事　annual events
会長　president
らいひん　a (distinguished, honored) guest,
　a visitor

はげます　to encourage
どれも　all
たいくつする　to be bored
〜えばいいと思う　to wish that〜
校歌　a school song
先頭に立つ　to take the lead
教科書　textbook

つ自分の名前を大きい声で言った。

　その晩、お祝いとして、お父さんが外に食事に

連れていってくれた。

—————— 第十七課　練習問題 ——————

I. A. 質問に答えなさい
1. 一年三組の教室には誰がいましたか。
2. 入学式はどこでありましたか。
3. 誰が入学式のあいさつをしましたか。
4. 式が終わってから生徒達はどこに行きましたか。
5. その晩、お祝いとしてみんなは何をしましたか。

B. True or False
1. 入学式の日はいい天気でした。
2. 教室の後ろには新入生が心配そうな顔をして立っていました。
3. 入学式は体育館でありました。
4. 大人の話はわかりやすかったです。
5. 入学式は校歌で終わりました。

II. 次の質問に答えなさい
1. あなたは入学式をどう思いますか。
2. アメリカにも入学式がありますか。
3. 日本の小学校の入学式に行ってみたいですか。それはどうしてですか。

—— Unit 17 Culture Notes ——

kyōshitsu

A Japanese classroom is more than a place for study. The children help serve hot lunches to their classmates there. They also sweep and mop their classroom at the end of the day.

kyōkasho

Textbooks are given to the students and become their own property. Each book is a thin, paperbound volume, and all books are easily carried home each day in the student's *randoseru*.

梅雨、失敗、お寿司

　六月になった。エィミーがアメリカに帰る日も近くなった。ゆっくりといつもの道を家に向かって歩いているうちに、突然さしていた傘がこわれてしまい、雨のしずくが顔にかかった。エィミーは傘をもう一度開こうとしたがぬれて歩くのも楽しいだろうと思った。日本での思い出をできるだけたくさん作りたいと思っていたので、そのまま歩き出した。

　梅雨時の細かい雨にぬれて歩いているうちに、思い出が次々に浮かんできた。この一年間に色々な事を学んだが、わからない事もまたずいぶん

梅雨　the rainy season*	かかる　to splash
失敗　a failure, a mistake	ぬれる　to get wet
向かう　to head toward	できるだけ　as much as possible
突然　suddenly	梅雨時　the rainy season
さす　to hold up (an umbrella)	細かい雨　misty rain　(細かい＝ small, fine)
傘　umbrella	次々に　one after another
こわれる　to be broken	学ぶ　to learn
しずく　a drop	

あった。失敗ばかりしてきたような気もした。

　たとえば、こんな事があった。ある日花屋でエィミーはきれいな花束を見つけた。お母さん、喜ぶだろうなと思いながらエィミーはその花束を買った。家に帰ってエィミーが差し出した花束を見てお母さんはおどろいたようだったが喜んでいるようには見えなかった。エィミーは日本には花を贈る習慣がないのかしらと思った。

　しばらくたってから、エィミーはその時お母さんにあげた花束は仏前用の特別のもので、生きている人に贈るものではなかったということを知った。エィミーはとても恥ずかしかった。お母さんは私を傷付けたくないと思って何も言わなかったんだわ。がまんしてくれたんだわ。きっと他にも

たとえば　for example
花屋　a florist
花束　a bouquet of flowers
差し出す　to present
贈る　to give (a gift)

仏前　before a mortuary tablet
　　(as an offering); see 仏だん*
生きる　to live
恥ずかしい　to be embarrassed
傷付ける　to hurt (someone's) feelings

たくさんがまんしてくれていることがあるんだろうな。私だって色々がまんしているけれど他の文化を学ぶことは本当にたいへんだわ、とエィミーは思った。

エィミーは家に帰って、傘立てに傘を立てた。明日傘を直さなくちゃとエィミーは思いながら家の中に入った。

エ：「ただいま。」

みんな：「お帰りなさい。」

母：「エィミーさん、大島さんを覚えているわね。この間散らし寿司を持ってきてくださった方よ。」

エ：「ええ、覚えています。」

母：「明日うかがいますって言っておいたから。お寿司のおけがまだあったわね。」

文化　culture
傘立て　an umbrella stand
直す　to mend
この間　the other day, recently

散らし寿司　vinegared rice mixed with finely cut vegetables and topped with strips of seaweed, egg, and sometimes cooked seafood
うかがう　to visit
おけ　a wooden tray or container

エ：「ええ、空のまま返しちゃいけないんですね。」

母：「よく覚えているわね。」

エ：「私がクッキーを作りましょうか。」

母：「そうね。じゃ、お手伝いしましょう。」

返す　to return, to give back　　　　クッキー　cookie(s)

———— 第十八課　練習問題 ————

I.　A.　質問に答えなさい
　1.　エィミーはどうして失敗ばかりしたような気がしましたか。
　2.　エィミーが花束を差し出した時どうしてお母さんはおどろきま
　　　したか。
　3.　お母さんは色々な事をがまんしましたか。
　4.　エィミーは傘を直しましたか。
　5.　エィミーとお母さんは誰の家に行きますか。

B.　True or False
　1.　神戸では梅雨は五月に終わります。
　2.　日本には花を贈る習慣がないとエィミーは思っていました。
　3.　エィミーのあげた花束を見てお母さんはがまんしてくれたと
　　　エィミーは思っていました。
　4.　大島さんはドーナツを持ってきた人です。
　5.　エィミーは大島さんの寿司おけにクッキーを入れて返します。

II.　次の質問に答えなさい
　あなたの住んでいる所には梅雨がありますか。何月ですか。

Unit 18 Culture Notes

tsuyu

The rainy season arrives in Kobe in June bringing light mists, mild showers, and high humidity. June, the first month of summer, is also when children replace their wool winter school uniforms with lightweight summer uniforms. After *tsuyu* is over, everyone tends to the effects of the humid, moldy conditions by airing out clothes, throwing away spoiled food, and doing a general housecleaning.

butsudan

This cabinet is a small shrine where offerings of food (such as rice), flowers, and incense are made to the spirits of deceased family members. The cabinet contains a statue or portrait of the Buddha and the family's ancestral tablets (*ihai*).

To avoid embarrassing Amy, Mrs. Yamashita did not tell her directly about the real use of the flowers.

第十九課 UNIT 19 大島家で

　翌日家を出ようとして傘を取ったエィミーは、傘が修理してあるのに気がついた。「お母さんが修理してくれたんだわ。自分でしなければいけなかったのに。」とエィミーは思った。

　お母さんとエィミーは、クッキーを持って、大島さんの家へ行った。大島さんは二人にお茶を出してくれた。エィミーは大島さんに「お口に合うかどうかわかりませんが。」と言いながらクッキーをわたした。「まあ、そんなに気を使ってくださらなくてもいいのに。これ、エィミーさんが焼いてくださったの。おいしそうだこと。じゃ、遠慮なくいただきます。」と大島さんは言った。

翌日　the following day
修理する　to repair, to mend
口に合う　to suit one's taste

～こと　this こと emphasizes its preceding
　phrase（female speech）
遠慮なく　without reserve, at ease

156

　三人はお茶を飲みながらしばらく話した。エィミーはお腹が空いていた。お母さんにはエィミーのお腹がグーグー鳴っているのが聞こえた。時計が十二時を打った。大島さんは「あら、もうこんな時間。お腹がお空きになったでしょう。」と言いながら台所の方へ出ていった。そして、お寿司を持って戻ってきた。「何もありませんけれど、どうぞ。」と大島さんは言ったが、大島さんがあらかじめお寿司を注文しておいてくれたのがエィミーにもわかった。エィミーはお寿司が好きだったから、とてもうれしかった。それなのにお母さんは「どうぞおかまいなく。すぐ失礼しますから。」と言った。大島さんは「そうおっしゃらずにどうぞ。本当に何もなくて申し訳ないんですけ

お腹が空く　to be hungry
お腹がグーグーと鳴る　(one's) stomach growls
時計　a clock
戻る　to come back, to return
あらかじめ　in advance
注文する　to order

どうぞおかまいなく　please don't put yourself to any trouble on my account
すぐ失礼しますから　(we're) leaving soon
おっしゃらずに　polite form of 言わないで
何もなくて申し訳ないんです...　I'm sorry I don't have much to offer

れど。」と言った。

　お母さんは私がお腹が空いているのを知っているんだし『はい、じゃお言葉に甘えて。』とか何とか言ってくれるといいんだけど、とエィミーは思った。それなのにお母さんは、「本当におかまいなく。早めに済ませてきましたから。」と言った。お母さんったら、どうしてそんなうそをつくのかしら。私達何も食べていないのにとエィミーは思った。

　大島さんはなおも重ねて「でも、エィミーさんは食べられるでしょう、まだ若いんだし。」と言った。その時エィミーのお腹がグーと鳴った。お母さんはエィミーの方を向いて「どうするエィミーさん、いただく。」と聞いた。エィミーは赤くなったが「そうですね、せっかくだからいただ

（お）言葉に甘えて　to accept a kind offer
済ませてきましたから　polite form for
　食べてきましたから
〜ったら　used after a person's name when

the speaker is irritated with that person
うそをつく　to fib
なおも重ねて＝またもう一度
向く　to turn toward

きましょうよ。」と言った。ああよかった、と心の中でエィミーは思った。

　三人はお寿司を食べながらエィミーの出発（しゅっぱつ）や梅雨のことを話した。

　大：「ねえ、エィミーさん、かびはいやでしょう。」

　エ：「ええ。」

　母：「家ではかんそうきを買おうかって言っているんですけど、どうでしょうね。」

　大：「あれがあると、ずいぶん便利でしょうね。」

　エ：「布団（ふとん）かんそうきのようなものですか。あれはいいですね。かわいたお布団（ふとん）で寝るのはとても気持ちがいいですから。」

　大：「本当にね。ところで、エィミーさんはい

出発　departure
かび　mold
布団かんそうき　a small machine like a
vacuum cleaner for drying futon

便利（な）　convenient
かわく　to dry

つアメリカへ帰るの。」

　エ：「今度の土曜日です。」

　母：「ああ、そうそう、それで思い出したけれど、今度の金曜日にエィミーのお別_{わか}れ会_{かい}をするんです。来ていただけますか。」

　大：「ええ、喜んで。」

（お）別れ会　a farewell party　　　　　喜んで　I'd be happy to ...

—— 第十九課　練習問題 ——

I. A. 質問に答えなさい
　1. 家を出た時エィミーは何に気がつきましたか。
　2. エィミーがクッキーをわたした時大島さんは何と言いましたか。
　3. どうして大島さんは寿司を注文しておきましたか。
　4. どうしてお母さんは「うそ」をつきましたか。
　5. 大島さんはエィミーのお別れ会に来ますか。

　B. True or False
　1. 大島さんの家に行った時エィミーはお腹がいっぱいでした。
　2. エィミーとお母さんは大島さんの家に行く前にご飯を食べました。
　3. お母さんは寿司を食べられなかったようです。
　4. 山下さんの家にはかんそうきがあります。
　5. エィミーのお別れ会は今週の金曜日です。

II. 次の質問に答えなさい
　友達の家で何か出された時「遠慮」したことがありますか。
　それはどうしてですか。

—————— Unit 19 Culture Notes ——————

Accepting Food

In situations outside family interactions, it is usually considered impolite to accept food on the first offer. Mrs. Yamashita knew Amy was hungry, but she was just being polite when she refused Mrs. Ōshima's offers.

第二十課 UNIT 20

日本を発つ

　日本での最後の一週間、帰るしたくやたくさんのパーティーでエィミーはとてもいそがしかった。アメリカにいる家族のためにお土産を買った。茶道部の人達がエィミーをお別れのお茶会に呼んでくれた。そしてお茶席用のせんすをくれた。留学生とそのホストファミリーのためのパーティーもあった。何人もの人がとても長い感傷的なスピーチをした。エィミーは他の留学生と一緒にアメリカと日本の歌を歌わなければならなかった。とても恥ずかしかったけれど、楽しくもあった。

　出発の前の晩、山下家では数人の友達を招いて

発つ　to depart
最後（の）　final
別れの茶会　a farewell tea ceremony
　　gathering
〜（に）呼ぶ　to invite

お茶席用　for tea ceremony use
せんす　folding fan
感傷的　sentimental
スピーチ　a speech
招く　to invite

164

エィミーのためのパーティーが開かれた。みんな
が飲んで食べて、アメリカと日本の事を話した。
お父さんがエィミーはこの一年間でとてもよく日
本の文化を理解したと言った。エィミーはそうは
思わなかった。お父さんはお世辞を言っている、
と思った。山下一家はエィミーに日本人形を贈っ
た。それはエィミーが前から欲しいと思っていた
ものだった。

　その晩は荷造りに時間がかかって横になった時
にはかなり遅くなっていた。「今晩でこの部屋で
寝るのも最後なんだわ。」と思いながら雨の音を
聞いているうちに、なみだが出てきた。日本での
初めての晩、窓の外の虫の声を聞いてどんなに
心細く思ったかをエィミーは忘れていた。エィミ
ーの頭にはもう二度と会えないかもしれない山下

理解する　to understand
（お）世辞を言う　to pay a compliment, flatter
人形　doll

荷造り　packing (a suitcase)
心細い　lonely and depressed
二度と〜ない　never〜again

家の人々の笑顔が次々に浮かんだ。

　翌朝、家族全員がエィミーを空港まで見送った。エィミーはとてもきんちょうしていた。みんなは悲しそうだった。エィミーはあまりにも日本に慣れてしまったので、アメリカの生活に溶け込めるかどうか心配だった。山下さんの家の人達に会いたくなるだろうなと思った。お母さんは「アメリカの家族のみなさんがお喜びでしょうね。」と何度も言った。とうとう飛行機に乗る時間になった。エィミーはみんなと最後のあいさつをかわした。

　エ：「お世話になりました。」

　父：「こちらこそ。」

　母：「エィミーさんがいてくれてとても楽し

笑顔　a smiling face
翌朝　the following morning
全員　all the members
空港　airport
見送る　to see (someone) off
悲しい　sad
溶け込める（と）〜　to adjust to〜

飛行機　airplane
（お）世話になりました　thank you for taking care of me
こちらこそ　literally, "me too." In this case, as a reply to お世話になりました, it means "You have taken care of me"

かったわ。」

一&明：「気をつけてね。アメリカに着いたらロックのテープを忘れないで送ってね。」

エ：「ええ、もちろん。一郎さんも明子ちゃんも忘れないでおまんじゅうを送ってね。」

まゆみはただ泣いているばかりだった。エィミーはまゆみを抱きしめて「泣かないでね。会いたくなったら私の顔を思い出してね。」とやさしく言った。まゆみにキスをしてエィミーは飛行機に乗り込んだ。

ロック　rock (music)
テープ　(cassette) tape
もちろん　of course
泣く　to cry

抱きしめる　to embrace (someone) tightly, to give a big hug
キスをする　to kiss
乗り込む　to board (a plane)

—— 第二十課　練習問題 ——

I. A. 質問に答えなさい
1. 日本での最後の一週間、エィミーは何でいそがしかったですか。
2. 留学生とそのホストファミリーのパーティーではみんながどんなことをしましたか。
3. 山下家のパーティーではどんなことがありましたか。
4. エィミーは最後の晩何をしましたか。どんな気がしましたか。
5. どうしてエィミーはアメリカの生活に溶け込めるかどうか心配でしたか。
6. エィミーが飛行機に乗り込む前にまゆみはどうしましたか。

B. True or False
1. エィミーは日本文化をよく理解したと思いました。
2. エィミーは早くアメリカに帰りたがっていました。
3. エィミーはあまり日本に慣れていませんでした。
4. みんなはエィミーがすぐアメリカに帰るからうれしかったです。
5. 一郎も明子もアメリカのロックのテープをほしがっていました。

II. 次の質問に答えなさい
あなたがエィミーだったら、アメリカに帰って一番初めに何がしたいですか。

Unit 20 Culture Notes

Farewells

Farewells, whether final or temporary, are important in Japanese culture. It is not uncommon for a host to see guests to their car and wave goodbye until they have driven out of sight. Likewise, if guests are taken to a train, the host will see them safely aboard and then watch the train depart.

Appendixes

MAKING ZARU SOBA (Unit 2)

(Serves 4)

INGREDIENTS

DIPING SAUCE
*2 cups bonito-flavored soup stock (dashi)**
4 Tbl. soy sauce
1 1/2 Tbl. mirin
2 Tbl. sugar

1 pound dried soba noodles
1 sheet nori, cut into thin strips
2 green onions, finely chopped
2 tsp. wasabi paste
5 Tbl. grated daikon

PREPARATION

Heat the dashi, soy sauce, mirin, and sugar for the dipping sauce in a sauce-pan until the sugar dissolves.

Chill the sauce.

Fill a large pot with cold water and bring it to a full boil while preparing the nori, onions, wasabi, and daikon.

Add 1 pound of dried *soba* noodles to the boiling water and stir gently. Return to a boil. Add 1 cup of cold water and return to a boil once more.

Pour the noodles into a strainer to drain. Set the strainer into a bowl of very cold water to chill and firm the noodles. Stir briskly for a few seconds, then rinse and drain.

Serve the noodles on *zaru* baskets or plates. Garnish with nori strips. Set out individual cups filled with dipping sauce for each person. Serve the onions, wasabi, and daikon in separate bowls so that students can season their own dipping sauce to taste.

_____

*For homemade dashi, refer to *The Book of Soba* (Unit 5 Culture Notes). Instant dashi can be purchased at Asian grocery stores. Follow the directions on the package.

173

MAKING KURI MANJŪ (Unit 4)

INGREDIENTS

(Makes 40–50)

FILLING
*1–2 cans sweetened red bean paste**

DOUGH
2 eggs
1/4 cup salad oil
1 cup sugar
2 tsp. baking powder
3 cups all-purpose flour (sifted)

mirin
soy sauce
1 egg yolk
white sesame seeds (optional)

PREPARATION

MAKING THE FILLING
Put the bean paste into a large bowl and stir to an even consistency. Spoon out a small portion (about 1/2 to 1 tsp.) and roll it into a ball. Prepare 40–50 balls, washing hands frequently to avoid sticking.

MAKING THE DOUGH
Beat the eggs gently; add oil, sugar, and baking powder. Add sifted flour a little at a time until the dough is very soft and pliable. (The Japanese say until the dough is "as soft as a baby's ear lobe.") It may not be necessary to use all 3 cups of flour.

Take a small amount of dough, and wrap the bean paste filling to form a rounded, oblong shape. The dough should cover the filling smoothly and evenly. Flattening the bottom gently, place the *manjū* on wax paper.

Mix a few drops of mirin and a *drop* of soy sauce with an egg yolk. (Too much soy sauce will cause discoloration.) Brush this mixture lightly along the very top of each *manjū*. White sesame seeds may also be sprinkled over the top.

Place the *manjū* on cookie sheets and bake at 350°F. for 20–25 minutes.

---

*Red bean paste is made from adzuki beans and can be purchased at Asian grocery stores.

"OSHŌGATSU" (Unit 12)

Words: 東 くめ
Music: 滝 廉太郎

<u>お正月</u>

もういくつねると　おしょうがつ

おしょうがつには　たこあげて

こまをまわして　あそびましょう

はやくこいこい　おしょうがつ

"SAKURA" (Unit 16)

Traditional Japanese Song

さくら

さくら、さくら

においぞいずる

やよいのそらは

いざや、いざや

みわたすかぎり

みにゆかん

かすみかくもか

GLOSSARY

Arranged according to the hiragana syllabary
(with unit numbers).

あ ▬▬▬▬▬

あいさつをかわす　to exchange greetings （14）

間（に）　while （3）

青い　blue （17）

（から）上がる　to get up out of （8）

あくびする　to yawn （5）

開ける　to open （4）

朝　morning （5）

足　feet, legs （8）

あずき　a kind of small red bean (adzuki) （3）

汗　sweat （1）

遊び場　a play area （6）

あたたまる　to warm oneself （9）

頭に浮かぶ　to occur to one's mind （11）

熱い　hot （8）

集まる　to gather （5）

あっという間に　all of a sudden （16）

甘い　sweet （13）

甘酒　a sweet drink made from fermented rice （13）

アメリカ式　American style （3）

あら　an exclamation of suprise (female speech) （12）

洗う　to wash （8）

あらかじめ　in advance （19）

表す　to show （2）

安全　safety, security （15）

案内する　to show around （3）

あんまり　emphatic form of あまり （14）

い ▬▬▬▬▬

言い残す　to leave something unsaid （10）

以外　outside of, other than （10）

生きる　to live （18）

生け花　flower arrangement* （3）

生ける　to arrange (flowers and such) in a vase （3）

以上　more than　(7)

いす　chair　(4)

忙しい　busy　(6)

一日中　all day long　(10)

一年生　first grader　(16)

一家　a household, a family　(1)

一行　a party (the "Yamashita party" or group)　(15)

一緒に　together　(8)

一生けんめい　as hard as one can, with all one's might　(10)

いったい　how on earth!　(5)

行ったものだ　used to go　(9)

祈る　to pray　(15)

居間　living room　(4)

いや　no　(9)

いやになる　to become tired of, averse to　(7)

いよいよ　at long last　(13), finally　(17)

いる　to need, to be necessary　(14)

色　color　(5)

色々　various　(5)

色々な思いをする　to have various experiences　(11)

（お）祝い（物）　a gift (for celebration)　(16)

う

ウイスキー　whiskey　(4)

うかがう　to visit　(18)

浮かぶ　to float　(4)

ウキウキする　to be cheerful and lighthearted　(16)

後ろ　behind　(6)

うそをつく　to fib　(19)

歌　a song　(12)

歌う　to sing　(12)

家中の者　all the family members　(13)

〜うちに　while〜　(16)

打つ　to strike, to hit　(13)

うながす　to prompt, to urge (someone to do〜)　(16)

うまくいく　to go well　(2)

〜（と）うまくいく　to do well with〜　(12)

売る　to sell　(15)

うれしい　happy　(4)

え

絵　a picture, a painting　(9)

英会話　English conversation　(11)

映画　a movie　(10)

ええと　um, well　(6)

笑顔　a smiling face　(20)

エスカレーター　escalator　(6)

〜えばいいと思う　to wish that　(17)

エプロン　apron　(8)

遠慮なく　without reserve, at ease　(19)

お ━━━━━━━

多い　many　(6)

おおい　hey!　(15)

大急ぎで　in a big hurry　(16)

大声で　in a loud voice　(5)

大きさ　size　(5)

大そうじ　a thorough house-cleaning　(12)

おおみそか　the last day of the year (New Year's Eve)　(12)

お帰りなさい　welcome home　(8)

お鏡 = 鏡もち　a round, mirror-shaped rice cake (an offering)*　(12)

おかし　sweet(s)　(4)

起きる　to get up out of bed　(5)

奥　the innermost part of the first floor behind the public shop area　(7)

置く　to put, to place, to have　(11)

屋上　a flat rooftop　(6)

送る　to send　(16)

贈る　to give (a gift)　(18)

おけ　a wooden tray or container　(18)

起こす　to wake (someone) up　(5)

押し入れ　a closet used mainly for the storage of futon　(3)

押す　to push, to press　(15)

おずおず（と）　hesitantly, nervously　(2)

おせち = せち料理　dishes for the New Year*　(12)

遅く　late　(11)

お茶席用　for tea ceremony use　(20)

おつかれさま　you must be tired (a polite greeting)　(8)

おっしゃらずに　polite form of 言わないで　(19)

お出かけ　（出かける）　(11)

男湯　the men's bath　(9)

落とす　to drop (something)　(2)

大人　an adult　(15)

おどろく　to be surprised　(14)

お腹がグーグーと鳴る (one's) stomach growls　(19)

お腹をすかす　to feel (get hungry)　(11)

お腹が空く　to be hungry　(19)

同じように　in the same way (同じ= the same)　(6)

覚える　to remember　(6)

思い　a thought　(4)

重い　heavy　(14)

思いが浮かぶ　thoughts come across one's mind　(4)

思い出す　to remember　(4)

思い出　recollections　(9)

おもちゃ　toy(s)　(6)

思わず　unintentionally, in spite of oneself　(8)

おやつ　an afternoon snack　(10)

オリエンテーション　orientation　(1)

おりる　to go down, to descend　(4)

おろす　to grate　(2)

終わり　an end　(8)

音楽　music　(11)

温度　temperature　(9)

女湯　the women's bath　(9)

か

外国人　foreigner　(6)

会社　a company　(11)

外人　foreigner (colloquial for 外国人)*　(6)

階段　stairs, staircase*　(3)

会長　president　(17)

買い物に行く　to go shopping　(5)

カウンター　counter (architectural structure)　(2)

返す　to return, to give back　(18)

顔　a face　(4)

かおり　fragrance　(16)

かがり火　bonfire　(13)

かかる　to hang　(3), リボンのかかる〜　〜to be tied with a ribbon　(16)

かかる　to splash　(18)

描く　to draw, to paint　(9)

家具　furniture　(6)

かけじく　a hanging scroll, cf. かけもの　(3)

かご　basket　(9)

傘　umbrella　(18)

傘立て　an umbrella stand　(18)

かざる　to decorate　(14)

〜方　a manner, a way, how to〜　(2)

カタカタする　to clatter　(11)

形　shape　(5)

がっかりする　to feel discouraged, to lose heart　(8)

活気に満ちる　to be full of spirit and life　(15)

カッコイイ　(it) "looks good," is fashionable　(11)

活動　activity　(10)

〜かどうか　whether or not〜　(1)

〜かな　(I) think, guess (wonder)〜　(9)

悲しい　sad　(20)

かなり　considerably　(15)

かばん　satchel　(16)

かび　mold　(19)

かぶせる　to put on (a hat)　(16)

壁　wall　(9)

カーペット　carpet　(4)

かまいません　it's o.k., it's all right

かまわないこと　an acceptable thing　（かまう = to mind, to care about, to be concerned about）(2)

がまんする　to endure, to exercise one's patience　(8)

神　god, God, divinity, divine being, spirit*　(12)

紙　paper

〜かもしれない　perhaps, maybe, might〜　(8)

通う　to attend school　(10)

空　empty　(5)

体　body　(8)

空手　karate　(a martial art)　(10)

〜がる　looks like〜, shows signs of〜　(4)

かわく　to dry　(19)

かわら　tile (for the roof)　(3)

考え事をする　to think about something　(10)

考える　to think　(5)

元日　New Year's Day　(14)

感傷的　sentimental　(20)

感じる　to feel　(7)

歓声をあげる　to shout for joy, to let out a cheer　(13)

き

黄色い　yellow　(5)

着がえ　changing clothes　(8)

着がえる　to change (into one's clothes)　(8)

気がする　to think, to have a feeling that　(11)

聞き入る　to listen attentively　(13)

きざむ　to mince　(2)

キスをする　to kiss　(20)

傷付ける　to hurt (someone's) feelings　(18)

着せる　to clothe, to dress　(16)

きっと　surely　(4)

気を使う　to care about, to worry about　(7)

気をつける　to be careful (12)

気になる　to get (something) into one's head to the point where one can't think of anything else　(2)

木のゆか　a wooden platform upon which the bather sits (ゆか = floor)　(9)

きびしい　strict　(7)

決める　to decide (on), to arrange　(7)

気持ち　a feeling　(7)

（お）客さん　customer(s)　(7)

キャッと叫ぶ　to yell, to cry out　(8)

急（な）　steep　(3)

きゅうくつ（な）　tight, cramped, uncomfortable (14)

教室　classroom　(17)

教育ママ　"education mother" (10)

教会　church　(15)

教科書　textbook (14)

兄弟　sibling(s)　(4)

京都　an imperial capital of Japan (A.D.794–1868), famous for its traditional architecture, gardens, and art　(16)

興味　an interest　(1)

切る　to cut　(14)

金色　gold color　(13)

近所　neighborhood　(7)

きんちょうする　to be tense (16)

く

空気　air　(12)

空港　airport　(20)

くぐる　to pass through, under (2)

クスクス笑う　to giggle, to chuckle (10)

果物屋　fruit store (7)

口に合う　to suit one's taste (19)

靴　shoes (3)

クッキー　cookie(s) (18)

くつろぐ　to relax and make oneself comfortable (14)

配る　to distribute (13)

組　class, group (17)

位　about, to the extent of (7)

クラス　class (17)

クラブ　club (10)

グルグル歩き回る　to walk around and around (16)

け

計画　a plan (5)

けいだい　the precincts, the grounds (15)

げたばこ　shoe cabinet (9)

玄関　an entrance way* (3)

元気が出てくる　to cheer up (4)

けんこう　health (15)

けんだま　a cup and ball game* (15)

こ

こい目　strong (as in taste or flavor) (2)

こう水　perfume (6)

校歌　a school song (17)

交換留学生　exchange student (1)

高校　senior high school (10)

校長先生　a principal (17)

紅白歌合戦　a singing competition between two teams called the "reds" and the "whites," broad cast every New Year's Eve on NHK, a major public television network (12)

好物　a favorite dish (food) (10)

声　a voice (a call of an insect) (4)

心が軽くなる　to feel relieved (11)

心細い　lonely and depressed (20)

午後　afternoon (p.m.) (10)

ゴシゴシ洗う　to give a good scrub (8)

ご心配なく　please don't worry (6)

答える　to answer (1,4)

こたつ*　(see Unit 13 Culture Notes)

こちらこそ　literally, "me too"; in this case as a reply to お世話になりました, it means "You have taken care of me" (20)

小包　a package (16)

〜こと　this こと emphasizes its preceding phrase (female speech) (19)

〜ことができる　can, be able to〜 (1)

〜ことにする　to decide to〜 (6)

〜ことになる　it is decided that〜, supposed to be that〜 (12)

ごとに　each (17)

言葉　word(s) (10)

（お）言葉に甘えて　to accept a kind offer (19)

粉　flour (2)

この間　the other day, recently (18)

この頃　nowadays (10)

ご飯　rice, a meal (5)

ご夫妻　Mr. and Mrs. (7)

こぼす　to drop (13)

細かい雨　misty rain（細かい = small, fine）(18)

困る　to be troubled (10)

衣　a priest's robe (13)

〜頃　about the time when〜 (9)

こわがる　to fear (6)

こわれる　to be broken (18)

今度こそ　surely <u>this</u> time (8)

さ ━━━━━━━━━

さ　indeed, you know (sentence-ending particle) (5)

さあ　well, come now (8)

最後（の）　final (20)

最初に　first (5)

サイズ　size (14)

（お）さいせん　a money offering (15)

材料　material(s) (9)

魚屋　a fish shop (7)

さがす　to look for (2)

先に　first (8)

桜　cherry tree (cherry blossoms)* (16)

酒　liquor (15)

叫ぶ　see「キャッと叫ぶ」

ささげる　to give (in a devotional sense) (15)

差し出す　to present (18)

さす　to hold up (an umbrella) (18)

冊　a volume (a counter suffix for books) (4)

さっぱりした　refreshed (8)

茶道部　tea ceremony club* (10)

さびしい　lonely (4)

ざぶとん　a floor cushion* (6)

皿　a plate, dish (5)

さらに　again (10)

さわる　to touch (6)

参加する　to participate (10)

三が日　the first three days of the New Year (12)

さんけいしゃ　visitors to a shrine or temple (13)

し

〜しかない　there is only〜 (2)

仕方がない　it can't be helped (8)

しかる　to scold (2)

しく　to spread out, to lay (something) down (3)

仕事　work　(10)

ししゅう　embroidery (4)

試食品　sample food products (6)

しずく　a drop (18)

自然に　naturally (16)

したくをする　to prepare for (16)

知っているように　I'm quite sure you know〜 (7)

失敗　a failure, a mistake (18)

質問　question (1)

失礼（な）　impolite, rude (8)

しばらくして　after a little while (11)

しばらくすると　after a while (17)

しばらくすれば　in a short time (11)

写真部　photography club (10)

ジャイアント　giant (6)

しゃてき　target practice (15)

（お）しゃべりする　to chatter, to gossip (9)

習慣　custom (7)

自由に　freely (13)

重箱 a tiered box traditionally made of lacquered wood or porcelain (12)

修理する to repair, to mend (19)

宿題 homework (10)

じゅく private school* (10)

出発 departure (19)

順番を待つ to await one's turn (15)

準備（を）する to make preparations (12)

しょう to carry (something) on one's back (16)

しょうが ginger (2)

紹介する to introduce (1)

小学生 a primary school student (16)

正月 the New Year (12)

上級生 an upper-class student (17)

商店 a shop, a store (7)

商店街 a shop-lined street, a shopping district (5)

食事をする to have dinner (a meal) (1)

食事中 during a meal (5)

食卓 dining table (14)

食料品 foodstuffs (6)

食器 tableware (6)

ショッピングセンター a shopping center (6)

初日 a first day (16)

除夜の鐘 a temple bell which rings out the old year on New Year's Eve (12)

白い white (16)

神社 a Shinto shrine (15)

親切 kind (6)

新入生 a new student (17)

新年 the New Year (14)

心配する to worry (1)

す

ずいぶん really (13)

数学 math (10)

数週間 several weeks (6)

スーツケース suitcase (3)

数人 several people, a few persons (2)

スーパーマーケット a super market (7)

～末 the end of～ (10)

スキップをする to skip (16)

過ぎる to pass (6)

～過ぎる　too～, せますぎる= too narrow, cramped (8)

少ない　a few (9)

すぐ失礼しますから　(we're) leaving soon (19)

すぐなくなります　to go away quickly (7)

すごい　amazing (6)

寿司　vinegared rice and fish (12)

鈴　a bell* (15)

スヌーピー　Snoopy (16)

スピーチ　a speech (20)

すべる　to slide, be slippery (2)

済ませてきましたから　polite form for 食べてきましたから (19)

済む　to end, to finish (15)

住む　to live in, to reside at (7)

澄む　to become clear (13)

スリッパ　slippers (3)

すると　just then (5)

ズルズルと音を立てて食べる　to make a slurping sound while eating (2)

すれば＞えば　if (2)

座る　to sit (4)

せ

～製　made in～ (4)

生活　life (6)

生徒　student ＋達 = students (10)

制服　a uniform (6)

世界中　all over the world (6)

せがむ　to badger (someome to do something) (15)

石油ストーブ　a kerosene heater* (10)

（お）世辞を言う　to pay a compliment, to flatter (20)

せっかく　with much trouble and effort (16)

せっけん　soap (8)

説明する　to explain (2)

せまい　narrow (6)

先日　the other day (6)

（お）世話になりました　thank you for taking care of me (20)

せんす　folding fan (20)

洗濯物　laundry (16)

銭湯　public bath* (9)

先頭に立つ　to take the lead (17)

全身 the whole body (9)

全然 totally ("not at all" with negative verb) (8)

そ

～ぞ "listen to me," "I'm telling you" (16)

そうじ cleaning (12)

相談する to discuss, to talk over (something with someone) (12)

(お)ぞうに a soup for New Year's morning consisting of small pieces of mochi and vegetables in a lightly seasoned broth (14)

底 the bottom (9)

そこに thereupon (10)

その間 during that time (6)

その一 part one (8)

そのうち soon, before long (7)

その通り just the same, just like that (8)

その二 part two (9)

そば buckwheat noodles (2)

そばがら buckwheat hulls (3)

そば屋 a noodle restaurant* (2)

ソファー sofa (4)

そよ風 a gentle breeze (17)

それでも however, but (10)

それなのに = それだのに nevertheless, in spite of this (8)

それに besides, and also (5)

それまで until then (4)

そろそろ soon (10)

た

たい a sea bream (a type of fish) (12)

体育館 gymnasium (17)

体育着 a gym uniform (16)

たいくつする to be bored (17)

たいしたもの a valuable thing, a treasure (16)

大切にする to value (something) (16)

タイツ tights (16)

たいてい usually (5)

台所 kitchen (5)

タイルばり tiled (ばり = covered, lined) (8)

タオル towel (8)

たおれる　to collapse, to fall
　(4)

（お）たがいに　with each
　other, mutually　(5)

〜たことがある　with a past
　tense verb = have had the
　experience of〜　(2)

滝　a waterfall　(6)

抱き上げる　to take up in
　one's arms　(13)

抱きしめる　to embrace
　(someone) tightly, to give a
　big hug　(20)

たくあん　pickled daikon
　(radish)　(5)

たしかに　certainly
　(14)

助け合う　to help one another
　(14)

たずねる　to ask　(8)　出す
　　to send　(6)

ただ　free　(6)

ただいま　I'm home　(8)

ただもう　emphasizes 知りた
　い

立つ　to stand　(5)

発つ　to depart　(20)

脱衣所　a dressing room　(9)

建物　a building　(15)

たとえ　although, even though
　(7)

たとえば　for example　(18)

楽しい　enjoyable　(6)

だまる　to be silent　(11)

ためいきをつく　to sigh　(10)

ために　in order for〜　(10)

だめよ．．．歩いちゃ =．．．
　　歩いてはだめ (14)

〜たり、たりする　to do such
　　things as〜　(10)

だるまおとし*　(15)

たんす　a chest of drawers　(3)

たんにんの先生　a teacher in
　　charge　(17)

だんだん　gradually　(8)

ち

地下　a basement　(6)

違い　a difference　(6)

地下街　an underground market
　(6)

近寄る　to come near　(6)

茶屋　a tea stand　(15)

茶わん　a rice bowl　(5)

ちゃんとする　to do well and
　　properly　(16)

中国　China　(6)

駐車する　to park (a car)　(15)

中年　middle age　(9)

注文する　to order　(19)

朝食　breakfast　(5)

ちょうせんする　to challenge (someone)　(15)

チョコレート　chocolate　(4)

散らし寿司　vinegared rice mixed with finely cut vegetables and topped with strips of seaweed, egg, and sometimes cooked seafood　(18)

散りかけの桜　falling cherry blossoms　(17)

つ ━━━━━━━━━

～(に)ついて　regarding～　(1)

ついてくる　to follow　(6)

つかる　to soak　(9)

つかれている　to be tired　(4)

使わずに = 使わないで　without using～　(8)

次々に　one after another　(18)

次に　after　(5)

次の　next　(5)

着く　to arrive　(1)

つく　to strike (a bell)　(13)

机　desk　(3)

机に向かう　to sit at one's desk　(6)

つぐ　to pour　(10)

つけ物　pickles　(5)

つける　to dip　(2)

～ったら　used after a person's name when the speaker is irritated with that person　(19)

続ける　to continue　(10)

包み　a package　(4)

包紙　wrapping paper　(16)

勤め　a duty, task (勤めをする = to attend to one's duties)　(13)

つまむ　to hold between (in this case, chopsticks)　(2)

冷たい　cold (not applicable to the weather)　(2)

つめる　to cram, to fill　(12)

つゆ　soup, broth　(2)

梅雨　the rainy season*　(18)

梅雨時　the rainy season　(18)

つるす　to suspend　(13)

連れる　to take with　(3)

て ━━━━━━━━━

出会い　an encounter, a meeting　(1)

～てある　has been～, is～　(3)

手を清める　to cleanse one's hands　(15)

ティーシャツ　T-shirt　(4)

ていねいに　carefully　(4)

～ているところだ　to be in the midst of doing something　(16)

～ているところだった　was in the midst of doing something　(16)

テープ　(cassette) tape　(20)

出かける　to go out　(7)

手紙　a letter　(6)

できるだけ　as much as possible　(18)

鉄　iron, steel　(9)

手伝う　to help, to assist　(8)

手にする　to hold in one's hand(s)　(10)

デパート　department store　(5)

手水や　a water basin*　(15)

～てみる　to try　(2)

寺　a Buddhist temple　(12)

店員　a clerk, a salesperson　(6)

伝統的　traditional, 伝統 = tradition　(3)

と

ドア　door　(5)

トイレ　toilet*　(5)

どうかしたの　is there anything wrong? cf.どうしたの　what's wrong?　(5)

どうぞおかまいなく　please don't put yourself to any trouble on my account　(19)

とうとう　at last　(12)

どうやって　how　(6)

道路　road　(6)

特別に　specially　(3)

時計　a clock　(19)

溶け込める　（と）　～ to adjust to～　(20)

床の間　an alcove for the display of art*　(3)

ところが　however　(8)

ところで　by the way　(5)

年こしそば　New Year's Eve buckwheat noodles*　(13)

として　as　(10)

年寄　an elder, an aged person　(9)

突然　suddenly　(18)

（三人）とも　all (three people)　(10)

鳥居 a Shinto shrine gateway* (15)

取り出す to take out (3)

取り除く to remove (12)

どれも all (17)

とんでもない no way! out of the question! not at all! (11, 14)

な ━━━━━━━━

直す to mend (18)

なおも重ねて＝またもう一度 (19)

仲よくできる、仲よくする to get along well with (1)

流す to wash off (4)

ながめる to stare out (the window) (6)

泣く to cry (20)

なつかしい to miss (something) fondly (8)

何もなくて申し訳ないんです… I'm sorry I don't have much to offer (19)

なべ a pot 大きいなべ＝cauldron (13)

波 wave(s) (15)

なみだ tears (4)

なやみ trouble, worry, fear (11)

～なら if～, then～ (1)

鳴らす to ring (a bell) (12)

並ぶ to line (a street) (7), to stand in line (13)

鳴る to ring (13)

慣れる to get used to

なんだか somehow (10)

何て（きれいなもよう） what a (pretty design) (3)

何度も many times (1)

に ━━━━━━━━

二階 second floor (3)

肉屋 a meat shop (7)

ニコニコする to smile radiantly, to beam (13)

～（に）ついて regarding～ (1)

荷造り packing (a suitcase) (20)

二度と～ない never～again (20)

日本食 Japanese cuisine (6)

日本間 a Japanese-style room* (3)

荷物 baggage (3)

入学式　an entrance cere-
　　mony (for school)　(16)

庭　garden, yard　(16)

人形　doll　(20)

にんじん　carrot　(14)

ぬ

ぬいつける　to sew on　(16)

脱ぎだす　to start to take off
　　(8)

脱ぐ　to take off　(3)

ぬりばし　lacquered chop-
　　sticks　(2)

ぬりわん　a lacquered bowl
　　(5)

ぬるい　lukewarm　(9)

ぬれる　to get wet　(18)

ね

ねぎ　green onion　(2)

ネクタイ　necktie　(6)

ねっしん（に）　eagerly　(3)

眠い　sleepy　(眠る to sleep)
　　(4)

眠そうに　sleepily　(11)

寝る　to sleep　(11)

年賀状　a New Year's card*　(15)

年始まわりの客　New Year's
　　guests　(15)

年中行事 annual events　(17)

の

ノート　a notebook　(a short-
　　ened form of ノートブック
　　(10)

のに　even though　(8)

のばす　to stretch out, to extend
　　(8)

のぼる　to go up　(10)

のり　paste, glue　(12)

乗り込む　to board (a plane)
　　(20)

乗る　to get on　(5)

のれん　a shop curtain*　(2)

は

はがす　to peel off　(12)

はきかえる　to change into; cf.靴
　　をはく　(3)

はき出す　to sweep out　(12)

はく　to put on, to wear (shoes) (5)

はげます　to encourage (17)

運ぶ　to carry (2)

はし置き　chopstick holder (14)

はじに付ける　to attach to an end (13)

パジャマ　pajamas (11)

パジャマのままで　while still in pajamas (11)

初めて　for the first time (1)

はずかしい　embarrassed, shy (2)

ばっかり　only, just (spoken form of ばかり) (10)

はっきりと物を言う　to speak frankly and openly (8)

初詣　the first shrine or temple visit of the year (15)

花形　flower-shaped (14)

話しかける　to address oneself to someone (10)

花束　a bouquet of flowers (18)

花見　cherry blossom viewing (16)

花屋　a florist (18)

はねつき　a game similar to badminton* (15)

払う　to pay (9)

はりかえる　to repaper (a *shōji*) (12)

貼る　to stick, to paste, to affix (12)

晴れる　to become clear (17)

ハロー　hello (6)

晩　evening (10)

番が来た　(her) turn came (13)

ハンカチ　handkerchief* (1)

番台　attendant's booth (9)

ハンバーガー　a hamburger (6

パン屋　a bakery (7)

ひ ━━━━━━━━

火をたく　to kindle a fire (9)

飛行機　airplane (20)

ひざ　lap (2)

ひしゃく　a dipper (made from materials such as bamboo, finely shaved wood or metal) (15)

美術品の展示会　an art exhibition (美術 = art) (6)

必要（だ）　necessary (9)

びっくりする　to be surprised (4)

一切れ　a slice (5)

一つ一つ　one by one （13）

一休みする　to take a short rest （12）

一人にしておく　to leave (someone) alone （7）

一人になる　to be by oneself （10）

ひも　a string, a cord （14）

百八回　one hundred and eight times （12）

開く（ひらく）　to open （4）

ビリビリと破る　to rip to shreds （16）

広げる　to open, to spread out （10）

ふ

ファーストフード　fast food （6）

（そんな）ふう　(that) way （11）

夫婦　husband and wife （1）

深い　deep （12）

フカフカ　soft, fluffy （3）

福　(good) fortune, luck, happiness, blessing （12）

ふく　to wipe （8）, to mop (wipe) up （12）

父兄席　seats for parents and siblings （17）

ふしぎ（な）　strange, mysterious （4）

富士山　Mt. Fuji （9）

二日　two days （12）

仏前　before a mortuary tablet (as an offering);* see Unit 18 Culture Notes

ぶつぶつと言う　to grumble, to complain （10）

物理　physics （10）

筆入れ　pencil case （16）

太っている　to be fat （4）

布団　Japanese-style bedding （3）

布団かんそうき　a small machine like a vacuum cleaner for drying futon （19）

風呂　a bath （4）

風呂おけ　a bathtub （4）

風呂に入る　to take a bath （4）

風呂場　bathroom (this term refers only to the place for bathing; toilets are in a separate room) （8）

文化　culture （18）

ふん水　fountain （6）

文房具　stationery, writing materials （16）

へ

ベッド　bed　(3)

部屋　room　(3)

ベル　a bell　(17)

へん　an area　(9)

便利（な）　convenient　(19)

ほ

（お）ぼうさん（=ぼうず）a priest, monk　(13)

ぼうし　a hat*　(16)

方へ　toward　(8)

ボーイスカウトの子供達　boy scouts　(13)

ボーッとする　to be "spaced out," in a daze　(10)

ホームシックにかかる　to get homesick　(12)

ホカホカ（の）　warm　(10)

ぼく　I (informal male speech)　(9)

ほこらしく思う　to feel proud　(14)

干す　to dry　(16)

ホストファミリー　host family　(1)

細長い　narrow and long　(8)

ホッとする　to feel relieved (8)

ほどく　to untie　(16)

ほとんど　mainly, mostly　(3)

ほとんど（の）　most　(9)

本でん　a main (inner) shrine (15)

本屋　a bookstore　(7)

ま

真新しい　brand new　(17)

（お）まいり　a visit to a temple (shrine), to worship (15)

まう　to flutter about, to dance (17)

まくら　pillow　(3)

まだ来たばかり　(you've) but just arrived　(11)

町　city, town　(6)

まっか　bright red　(8)

まど　window　(6)

学ぶ　to learn　(18)

まねをする　to imitate　(8)

招く　to invite　(20)

迷う　to be in doubt　(10)

丸太　a log　(13)

まるで　as if（16）

まわり　surrounding（13）

（お）まんじゅう　a bun with bean jam filling（one type of Japanese sweet）（14）

み ▬▬▬▬▬▬▬▬▬

実　a seed（2）

見送る　to see（someone）off（20）

店　a store（6）

みそしる　miso soup（5）

道　a path, a street（7）

見つかる　to be found out（2）

見つける　to find（10）

みどり色　green（5）

（お）みやげ（土産物）souvenir(s)*（3, 15）

む ▬▬▬▬▬▬▬▬▬

向かう　to head toward（18）

向く　to turn toward（19）

向こうがわ　the other side（2）

虫　insect（4）

むしあつい　hot and humid（1）

むね　the chest（4）

むねがいっぱいになる　（one's）chest becomes filled with emotion（4）

むらさき　purple（13）

め ▬▬▬▬▬▬▬▬▬

目をこする　to rub one's eyes（11）

目を覚ます　to be awake（11）

（お）めでたい　happy, joyous, propitious（12）

めん（めんるい）　noodles（2）

も ▬▬▬▬▬▬▬▬▬

もえる　to burn（13）

モール　mall（7）

もちろん　of course（20）

もどる　to come back（10）

〜もの　because（3）

ものすごく　terribly（8）

もよう　design, pattern（3）

門　gate（3）

問題　question(s), problem(s)（1）

や

八百屋 a vegetable store (7)

やがて before long (11)

焼きいも a baked sweet potato＋屋 = a sweet potato vendor * (10)

焼き魚 broiled fish (5)

焼き物 pottery (1)

野球 baseball (10)

やけど a burn (9)

やさしい soft, gentle (4)

屋台（店） an open air stall, a booth for selling things (15)

やって来る to come (1)

やっと at last (1)

屋根 a roof (3)

やはり after all, as suspected (10)

ゆ

湯 hot water (8)

ゆかた an informal, lightweight cotton kimono for summer wear; a bathrobe (8)

夕涼みする to enjoy the cool evening (breeze) (9)

湯船 a bathtub (8)

夢 a dream (11)

夢を見る to dream (11)

よ

〜用 use of〜 (5)

用意する to prepare (3)

洋式 western-style (5)

ようちえん kindergarten (10)

〜ようにする to do (something) in such a way that〜, to make sure that〜 (12, 15)

〜ようになる to come to do〜, to come to be that〜 (8)

用品 supplies (4)

洋服だんす a wardrobe （洋服 = western-style clothes）(3)

翌朝 the following morning (20)

翌日 the following day (19)

横に along side, next to (6)

横になる to lie (down) (4)

〜（に）呼ぶ to invite (20)

夜 night (11)

寄る to approach, to gather (at) (15)

喜^{よろこ}ぶ to be happy (1)

喜^{よろこ}んで I'd be happy to ...
　　(19)

呼^よんでほしい／てほしい＝ても
　　らいたい (1)

ら

らいひん a (distinguished,
　　honored) guest, a visitor
　　(17)

楽^{らく}なかっこう comfortable
　　dress (clothing) (10)

ランドセル a sturdy leather
　　knap sack used for books*
　　(16)

らんぼうする   to be rough
　　(16)

り

理解^{りかい}する to understand (20)

リボン ribbon (16)

理由^{りゆう} a reason (14)

両側^{りょうがわ}（に） (on) both sides, ei-
　　ther side (7)

料金^{りょうきん} a charge, a fee (9)

両親^{りょうしん} parents (4)

料理^{りょうり} cooking, cuisine (11)

りんとした   clear and crisp (13)

れ

例^{れい} an example (8)

（お）礼^{れい}を言^いう to express
　　thanks (4)

歴史^{れきし} history (10)

列^{れつ}を作^{つく}る to line up (13)

練習^{れんしゅう}する to practice (1,2)

連絡^{れんらく}する to inform, to notify
　　(7)

ろ

廊下^{ろうか} a hallway (17)

ロープ a rope (13)

ロック rock (music) (20)

わ

（お）別^{わか}れ会^{かい} a farewell party
　　(19)

別^{わか}れの茶会^{ちゃかい} a farewell tea cere-
　　mony gathering (20)

別^{わか}れる to separate (9)

〜（と）別^{わか}れる   to part from
　　(2)

ワクワクする to get excited
  (13)

〜わけじゃない it's not that〜,
  it's not because〜 (10)

〜わけにはいかない there's no
  way〜 (9)

災_{わざわ}い misfortune (12)

忘_{わす}れ to forget, to leave behind
  (5)

わたす to hand over (16)

わなげ ringtoss (15)

和_わ風_{ふう} Japanese-style (5)

笑_{わら}う to laugh (2)

ワンピース a one-piece dress
  (16)

WRITING PRACTICE

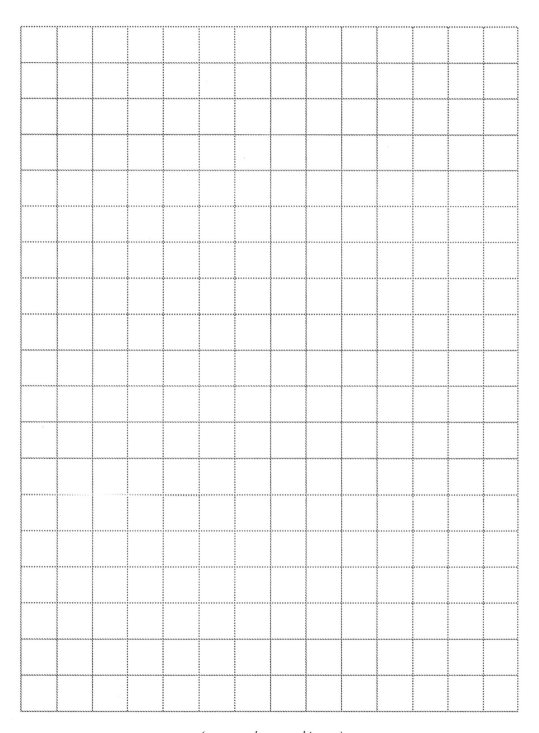

(you may photocopy this page)

WRITING PRACTICE

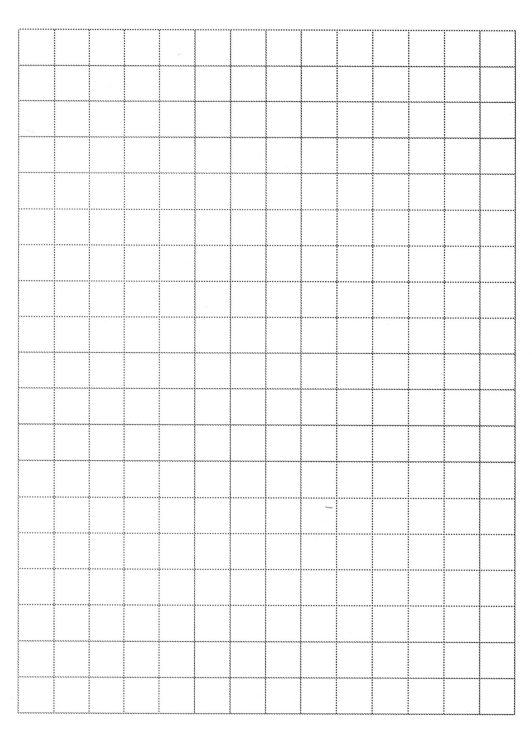

WRITING PRACTICE

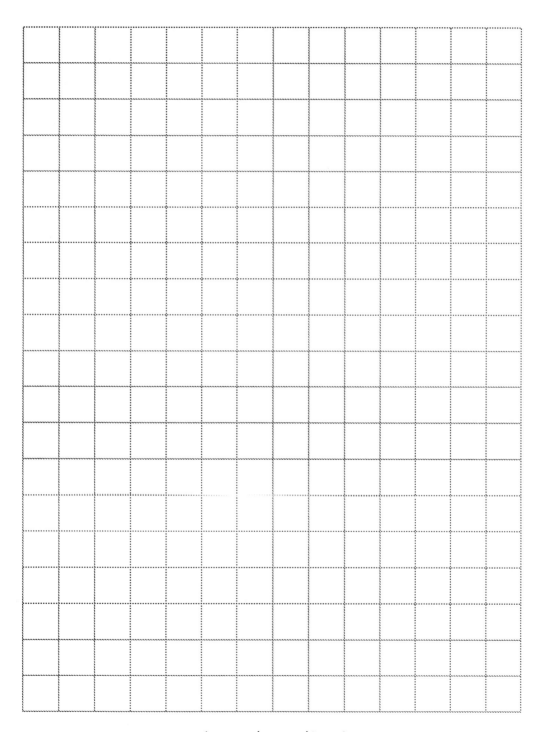

(you may photocopy this page)

To receive information about other Stone Bridge Press books and materials
on Japan and learning Japanese, contact:

STONE BRIDGE PRESS
P.O. Box 8208
Berkeley, CA 94707
U.S.A.
tel 510-524-8732 • fax 510-524-8711